Sweet Days & Beyond

Sweet Days & Beyond

THE MORSE FAMILY

EIGHT GENERATIONS OF MAPLE SUGARING

By
Burr Morse

HISTORICAL PAGES COMPANY

188 Main Street, Poultney, Vermont 05764

Published by the HISTORICAL PAGES COMPANY
188 Main Street, Poultney, Vermont 05764
Website at: www.historicalpages.com

First Edition
Text copyright © 2005 Burr Morse
Book Design: Penny H. Sheehan
Cover Design: Bill Loring
Front Cover Photo: Linda Hogan
*This is the sugarhouse of Burr's great-great grandfather, John Morse. It is in
Calais, Vermont, and is still being used every spring by Stanley Morse, a cousin.*
Back Cover Photo: Donald G. Lockhart, Perceptions, Inc., Charlotte, VT
Morse Farm Maple Sugarworks, website at: www.morsefarm.com

ISBN 0-9772692-1-3

PRINTED IN THE UNITED STATES OF AMERICA

Printed by Journal Press, Inc.
Poultney, Vermont
OCTOBER 2005

This book is dedicated to my father, Harry Morse.
Thanks for needing my help, Dad. I never said this in all those years that we worked together, but all things are better because of you, especially music, art, and writing. Sometimes it is hard, darn hard, but that's okay because I love what I'm doing. I love my roots. I love the smell of the sugarhouse, and remembering your stories and your love of life. You never did make me an optimist, but that's okay, too. I know I'm a work in progress. Thanks for needing my help, Dad.
I want you to know that I am dedicating this book to you.
—Burr

TABLE OF CONTENTS

A Trip to Hardwick • Air Enhancement in Vermont
Munger's Magic • Hang Gliding in the Pea Field
You Gotta be a Little Nuts • Tar Baby Vermont Style
Henry Ford Meets Bill Gates • Frost Heave Therapy
Give Pease a Chance • The Demographics of Varmints
Elm Planks with an Attitude • Space Age Cows
Houdini Returns

Into Fall

Life in the "Slow" Lane • Bus Season
Maple Peace • Signs of the Times
Gimpy Goblin • Deer Season
The Night Blooming Cereus • Regal Wreaths
Tessa and the Spice of Life • The Balloon Lady
Music for Better or Worse • Deep Roots Back Home
Animal Power Personified

Into Winter

Return to Spring

Dot Morse's Tribute Letter

Epilogue

State of Vermont
OFFICE OF THE GOVERNOR

Dear Readers,

What does it mean to be a 'real Vermonter'? As Governor of Vermont, this is a question I am often asked.

A real Vermonter is someone who has embraced the heritage of Vermont and in some way put his or her own unique stamp on it. The final stage in the attainment of 'real Vermonter' status is an understanding of one's self as part of something much larger and very special, coupled with a fierce pride in the things that make Vermont such a special place.

Burr Morse is someone who meets all of these criteria, and someone I am proud to call a friend. There is often much more to a real Vermonter than meets the eye, and at one time it was known as being a 'Renaissance Man.' Burr is a seventh-generation Vermonter who is a farmer, sugar maker, entrepreneur, marketer, newspaper columnist, jazz musician, and one of the greatest assets Vermont has. As hard as Burr works to promote his own business, he unfailingly gives equal time to promoting Vermont tourism and the Vermont maple industry.

Each year, Burr welcomes thousands to the Morse Farm Sugar Works and Cross Country Center just outside of Montpelier, Vermont's capital. Usually, they all leave with some maple syrup, kettle corn, or the happy afterglow that can only come from a recently-consumed maple creemee.

Much more importantly, however, they leave with a genuine experience they will never forget. They have a deeper understanding of the hard work and dedication it takes to be a farmer or sugar maker in Vermont. They see that it takes a special kind of person to weather adversity without becoming discouraged and to be a success while remaining true to your roots and who you are as a person. In short, they know they have finally met a 'real Vermonter.'

A gifted marketer, talented performer and natural showman, Burr is at the same time very humble and self-effacing and will likely be embarrassed about what I have written about him. Every word is true, however, and I wish him success, especially with this book, one of his most recent endeavors.

A trip through the pages of this book will be as close to getting to know someone as you can come without actually meeting him. However, once you have read this book, you will want to 'see the movie' and meet Burr in person.

Sincerely,

James H. Douglas
Governor

10

ACKNOWLEDGMENTS

This book has been my dream for a long time, and I have a long list of folks to thank for their help and support. Without them, it would have been like making maple syrup without the trees. Top on my list is Betsy, my chief confidant, soul mate, and purveyor of common sense and all things positive. Rob and Tom are chips off this old block. They took my music and made it better. They do for their grandparents and come home often. What more can you ask? Thank you, Mother Dot. You're the world's best mother. I was your student in the Morse School, and I'll never forget your energy and creativity. Thank you Elliott, Tick, and Susie— siblings supreme! Thanks to my 2001 buddies: Claude and Carolyn Stone, Ben Tomb and Jim Morse. Thanks to Steffen Parker, my editor and sugarhouse buddy. Thanks to Elaine and Stanley Fitch for trusting me with their photographs and David Aiken and Linda Hogan for their photographic genius. Thanks also to Betty Ann and Don Lockhart from Perceptions, Charlotte, Vermont.

To Jonathan Draudt, we are most grateful for your photographic knowledge and resourcefulness. Thanks to Marne Rizika for her tractor illustration. Thanks also to Bill Loring for his cover design. Thanks to editors: Peter Campbell-Copp and Don Wickman of the Historical Pages Company. Thanks to Chuck Colvin and the folks at the Journal Press. Very special thanks to Penny H. Sheehan for her design expertise. Thanks to my first editors Kathryn Mathieson and Eleanor Ott, whose editorial support started with a "sugarhouse talk." Thanks to my e-mail pals: Cousin Janie Morse, Cousin Julie Schafer, Al, Digger and all those supporters of *News from Vermont*. Thanks to all my music friends and Martha for the prayers. I love you, Russian Family. Thanks to my wonderful staff. Finally, thanks to everyone who comes to Morse Farm. *You folks are great!*

PROLOGUE

Hello, my name is Burr. Folks are always wondering how I got my name and if it's a family name. I say I can't think of a single "Burr" in my past, future or under my saddle—well let's just say it's not a family name. The Morse family lore on how I got my name starts in the early hours of March 16, 1948. It was snowing hard, blowing sideways, God-all-mighty cold kind of March morning. That kind of spring weather can happen here in Vermont, but don't plan on it. In fact, never plan on the weather in Vermont. It might be drizzly, muddy, overcast, and even occasionally nice. If it's spring in Vermont, you take what you get. My family was living up on the hill overlooking Curtis Pond and Maple Corner so when my mother said "It's time," my father started Grandpa Morse's 1946 Hudson and headed it down County Road toward Montpelier. Close to where the Morse Farm Maple Sugarworks now stands, Dad almost left the road. He might as well have dropped me off there because that's where I've spent most of my life. But being a Vermonter, he fought the wheel, won, and continued on to Heaton Hospital.

Mother got settled into a room to begin the long waiting and pacing till my birth. She went to the window and peered out at the weather. "Burrrrrr!" she muttered, shaking her head from side to side and I had my name. You know, I've always felt lucky to have that name. Had the weather been showing one of its other sides, she might have scrunched up her face and said "yuck!"

The slightly more believable tale from my mother is that my sister, Susie, gave me that name because she was only three when I was born and couldn't say "baby brother." She shortened it to "Burr."

Harry is my real name; Harry I. Morse, Jr., but "Burr" stuck because there already was a Harry Morse at home, my father, Harry Sr. Before the two of us, there was Sydney, Harry A., John, James II, and James I—seven generations of Morse Family farmers and maple sugarmakers right here in Central Vermont. I'm very proud of my heritage and especially the fact that my boys, Rob and Tom, generation number eight, share my love of maple sugaring.

Throughout this book, I'll talk about farming and sugaring as though they are one and the same because, well, they are. There are many words one can use to describe farming in Vermont but 'easy' is not one of them. We have rocks, ledges and a devilishly short growing season; throw in a dash of Murphy's Law and you have the full recipe. Every cloud has a silver lining, however, and for Vermonters that lining is maple sugaring. Sugaring is necessary to the personality of a Vermont farm. Without it, Morse Farm would be long gone and I might be selling insurance for a living. Sugaring (sugarin' to be exact) brings purpose and action to spring, economy to Vermont, and focus to this book, *Sweet Days and Beyond*.

Sugarin' is a fascinating process, only done in a very small region of the world. Sure, there are a few other states where maple syrup is made, but we, here in Vermont, get most of the attention because we make the best syrup. A Vermont sugarhouse, second only to the general store, is a gathering place—a focal point for pointless jabber and sweet triviality. My fifty-four sugaring seasons have found me in that steamy place with my ears open. Like the versions of how I got my name, the sugarhouse holds both truth and lore.

Being in the maple business, I meet a lot of folks who are interested in sugarin'. I divide them into two groups: those who have sugarin' in their DNA and love it like I do, and those who have heard about it and want to learn more. Both groups hunger not only for the gastronomic pleasures of our world-class product, but to enjoy the complete maple sugarin' experience. To serve the latter purpose, I decided to write this book. My intention was to rise above a dry narrative of "how, when, where and why," and go the extra mile—it's just kinda the Vermont way. Originally the book was to be titled *Sugarhouse Talk*, as in the "talk" about the history and process of sugarin' plus the "talk" of interesting anecdotes and lore (after all, B.S. doesn't always stand for "best syrup," you know).

So one frigid January day I sat down and started writing. I began with the Native Americans and progressed to more modern times, drawing from my memories and the stories of those who came before. I mingled the lore into my text with an eye toward proper flow and consistency. Seven generations of sugarin' heritage made my job easy, but I also found I had a natural inclination to write. Soon I was writing more than just my sugarin' book; I was writing bi-weekly newsletters for my e-mail list which I called *News from Vermont*. That, thanks to a good friend on that list, turned into a bi-weekly column in our local newspaper called *Burr's Whittlings*. I received a lot of great comments on the things I wrote. The most common one of all was, "you've got to write a book."

Sugarhouse Talk was finished last year and I considered having it printed for those folks who "hunger for more maple." By then there were fifty issues of *News from Vermont* and a little voice began suggesting that they too belonged in my book. Then it struck me—Vermont, as well as being the World epicenter for maple syrup, is the epitome of four seasons. Since spring, the king of seasons, was mostly covered with *Sugarhouse Talk*, why not let my *News from Vermont* stories serve the other three seasons? That idea fit like a glove on a frosty March morning as my bi-weekly newsletters parallel, speak to, and address each of the seasons.

Sweet Days and Beyond, like our famous four grades of maple syrup, covers it all; satisfying that universal hunger for more maple and throwing in a generous helpin' of each of Vermont's wonderful seasons. So join us as we start sugarin' season, trudge with us into the sugarbush, and then grab a chair by the evaporator for a four season Vermont experience full of sweet (and sometimes sour or bittersweet) tales. Happy reading! 🍁

(David Aiken Photo)

Early Sugarin': Fact and Family

Vermont was blessed with sugar maples, sugar weather, and the sugarin' frame of mind long before the English and French began boasting of their New World sugarin' heritage. More than likely, Algonquin Indians discovered the art of maple sugarin' by accident, finding purpose for the sweet sap from a wounded tree. The legend goes...

Shoshqua was hunting one late winter day, the time of year when the nights are still crisp and freezing but the snow softens with daytime thawing. That was the time when people of the Great North Woods felt enlivened by the promise of a new season. Earlier, a wet snow had fallen and many of the trees were bent or broken. As Shoshqua approached one particular tree, he noticed clear water dripping from a wound. It had been dripping so long that a deep, funnel-shaped hole had formed in the soft snow under the wound. He went

there, cupped his hands and drank the cold liquid. Thirst quenching, slightly sweet but not sticky, it was much like water, tree water. He was surprised to find the tree still dripping when he returned the next day.

Returning another day, he placed a water vessel under the drip while he hunted. By day's end, the vessel was overflowing. He took it back to the village where his mother Lamphu used the sweet liquid to boil the venison. Seeing that most of it boiled off as steam that first day, she asked Shoshqua to bring more of the tree water as the venison needed more tenderizing. When the meat was finally done, it lay in thick syrup. The venison had a new, sweet taste and the strange syrup tasted great as well. For his discovery, Shoshqua won the heart of Mahia, the prettiest maiden in the village. His people prepared venison that same way from then on, but only in that short time of year when the sweet tree water drips.

They gashed the sugar maple trees to wound them and gathered the sap in birch bark containers. Their method of boiling was long and arduous; having no metal containers, they super-heated rocks in hot coals and used deer antlers to transfer them into vessels of sap water. They repeated the process until the sap was sufficiently boiled down. Maple sugar was the end result, not syrup. By boiling sap even more than we do today to produce syrup, then cooling and stirring it, rock hard sugar was formed. It served the Indians' sweetening needs for an entire year.

My ancestors arrived in Vermont in the late 1780s from Massachusetts. James

Morse I must have made a wrong turn in Portland; many Morses went to Maine or further up into the Maritimes. James I, however, settled in Cabot, Vermont at a time when there were no roads (Heck, Vermont was still a Republic!) and Indians still primarily inhabited the area.

I was a Justice of the Peace (J.P.) in East Montpelier and recall a story about my great-great-great-great grandfather, James Morse I, who was the first J.P. of Cabot, and took his position very seriously. James had recently arrived in this new place when he summoned his young son, David. "Davey, come hither and to the forest we shall go."

John Morse 1815–1895, grandson to James, who first came to Vermont.

"What errand have you, father?"

"I have been appointed Justice of the Peace for this area of Cabot and one of my duties is to perform the rite of Holy Matrimony. I wish to practice this rite by marrying you to yonder tree stump."

"Yes, father, I am at your service."

James performed the ceremony as though it were a real marriage, to an embarrassed son. David, always the joker, spoke up, "Father, I will love and obey my new bride and if we bear fruit, I promise to provide the proper nurturing."

To this, James Morse stiffened and the sternness on his face said it all. "We do not discuss procreation, even with a tree."

As a J.P. in modern times, I have performed marriage ceremonies on inner tubes floating in a body of water and in tree houses. I have been asked to marry couples of the same or opposite sex, and have performed the rite several times

The Old West Church where Burr performed duties as Justice of the Peace. (Linda Hogan Photo)

The lady with her hand on Lewis Bancroft's shoulder is Burr's great-great-grandmother, Jane Bancroft Giddings.

with the couple's baby present as witness. The passage of time has brought many a change to this Vermont.

Vermont was a wild place back in old James Morse's time. Why in the world would he leave Massachusetts for the unknown North? We have no record of his travel, what route he took or how hostile the natives were. We suspect he learned the process of sugarin' from Vermont's Indians, which would indicate old James had a way with them. In spite of stories of his stoicism, he must have had a way behind closed doors, too; he sired seven children. James I died in Cabot in 1812.

I descended from one of those seven, James II, who moved from Cabot to Calais, VT. James II married Lucy Bliss and homesteaded about a mile west of Calais' County Road up toward Ellis Hill. Being a second generation Vermonter, he was a seasoned sugarmaker and was credited with not only starting the long line of Calais Morses, but also with continuing the even longer line of serious Morse sugarmakers.

Knowing that a new church was being planned over by Bliss Pond, James II requested that he and Lucy be buried at the Morse homestead on Ellis Hill when they died and that they be exhumed and reburied behind the church some day. That church, now called the Old West Church, was completed in 1823, and his family carried out James' wishes. As the story goes, when they disinterred and examined his body they found that he had a double row of teeth on both his upper and lower jaw. I asked fellow Calais resident and retired dentist, Alden Belcher, if this story might have been true. He said that if baby teeth don't fall out, it could happen.

James Morse II was an empire builder. His handiwork can still be seen up at the Morse settlement in Calais. His son John's sugarhouse is still being used today by my cousin, Stanley Morse. It's safe to say that whenever old James Morse II took on a project, he "really sunk his teeth into it!"

Homesteading in Vermont was hard work back in those days. A contemporary large farm consisted of twelve milking cows. Vermonters kept other animals and grew most of their staples. From the beginning, sugarin' was a mainstay of their farm life. Many of our present day sugarbushes had their origins from this same period. One never plants a good sugarbush; a good sugarbush is wild sugar

The days of homesteading, Elmina Spear Swazy, a Morse ancestor.

maples that have been thinned out over the years. Vermonters selected dominant maple trees and culled the weaker trees. They also thinned out other trees so the woods became nearly 100% maples. Repeated trimming of future generations left these areas looking much like orchards. Thus the term sugarbush, or maple grove, came to be.

The rigors of winter and everyday

Getting out in the sugarwoods in the old days.

Snow roller pulled by triple team.

Kids atop snow roller.

farming back then meant spring's onset of sugarin' was daunting. Often they prepared for the season with four feet of snow on the ground and drifts more than twice that high. My grandmother, Mildred Morse, wrote about snow rollers, the mainstay for maintaining public roads in her day:

> *"Among my earliest memories of life on the ancestral farm in Calais was of the period when snow was packed down and traveled over instead of being plowed off the roads. Living on a hill farm in those days meant we were among the last to be reached*

after a storm. I remember the joy my sisters and I felt when we heard the bells in the distance and then the creaking and squeaking of the huge red painted snow roller coming up the hill. We would rush to the windows and breathe holes in the frost so that we might see the horses as they came into view—four after a normal storm with sometimes six or even eight required to pull the big drums after a big snow-fall. The men, hunched over in their fur coats, caps pulled over their ears and tippets wound around their collars, would pull into our yard and pause hopefully by the door. On rare occasions my father would invite them in to have a pitcher of cider. Mother, however, disapproved of this. 'Hard cider was used in our house only in the practice of making vinegar!'"

Burr's sister, Susan Shattuck, mirrors her grandmother's seasonal spirit in the poem, "Winter."

My ancestors adapted to the harshness of their chosen region. They did what needed to be done and each year, without fail. During the short period of time between the beginning of snow melt and the swelling of maple buds, they harnessed the natural resource that sweetened the rest of the year. For most Vermonters, sugarin' is much more than an avocation. It is a rite of passage; the passage from winter's stagnation to the springing forth of buds and leaves and green

Typical conveyance to the sugarhouse, Raymond Wheeler driving "Prince," "Teddy" on seat.

grass—life—sometimes even human life.

My friend Robert Howrigan, of Fairfield, Vermont, said sugarin' kept his grandfather alive for years:

"My grandfather was crippled up with rheumatism and asthma. Several years there, he almost died in the winter, but something made him wait. I think it was sugarin'. When sugarin' started, they'd draw him up to the sugarhouse on a double sled and when he got into that steam, he'd be good for another year. I think he'd still be alive had it not been for a late sugar season!"

Animals, Snow, and Machinery

Winter is the time for contemplation in Vermont. We do our barn chores and keep an eye toward the next season. We plan for the upcoming sugar season, the king of all seasons for a Vermont sugar farmer.

Thoughts of sugarin' bring all the mystery and nervous anticipation of a ball game: who will prevail, nature or the sugarmaker? Will we go into overtime or will we get rained out? Will the sap be sweet or watery this year? How do we deal with all that snow? A crystal ball would be the perfect tool for a sugarmaker's pre-season, but for most of us, a foreboding would be ignored. We'd sugar anyway.

Late winter crust, strong enough to hold up the car. Harry Morse, circa 1937.

Mother Nature teases us with her late February weather. Day temperatures flirt with thirty-two degrees, softening the snow, but the nights are still and crisp.

Crunch, crunch, go our footsteps those late winter mornings and there is a different feel to the air. Winter's thoughts and plans now turn into actions. We use those warmest of February days to go to the sugarbush and break out roads so that horses or tractors can navigate. Buckets, covers, and spouts must be hauled into the woods, along with the gathering tank. This is a feat in itself during those years with nature's full eighty inch allotment of snow. We have not used horses at Morse Farm since 1948. I missed out on that experience. My father, Harry, related some of the nostalgia:

> *"Used to have a good team and a poorer one in reserve —
> had to work 'em all winter. It wasn't just a matter of
> keeping 'em fed so they'd be around for sugarin'. Horses
> are like people. They need exercise or they'll get fat. We'd*

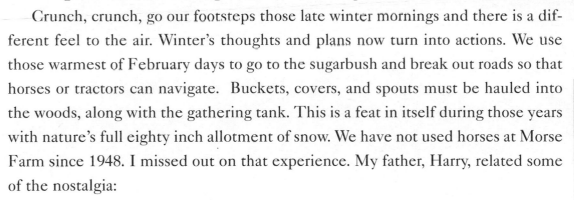

Snow "like we used to get."

*Gathering sap behind horses,
circa 1933.*

go out with 'em after every snow storm and walk over the sugar roads. You know, those roads have to be broke; you can't expect a horse to wallow through three feet o' snow. Sometimes we'd even have to shovel places where it drifted.

I've just loved sugarin' all my life from the time I was old enough to look over the edge of the pan. Horses get right into the spirit o' sugarin'. You talk to 'em, whether it's English or French, a few cuss words thrown in, they understand. A good team makes sugarin' a lot easier but that's not guaranteed: One time the Persons' boys were returning from the sugarhouse with five milk cans full o' syrup, their whole crop. The horses spooked just as they were crossin' the brook. All five o' those cans dumped over and the boys watched their hard work run west, toward Lake Champlain—said they'd never sugar again, and they never did!

We later used tractors. Tractors are a little like horses. They can't wallow through too much snow. We used to have an old Allis Chalmers HD-7 bulldozer that we'd break out the sugar roads with. One time we got the thing stuck in a six-foot drift. With all the thrashin' around we finally threw a track and had to get down in under it to shovel snow and pry the thing back on. My son, Elliott, was workin' on it at the time. Elliott had just got out from under it when the snow gave way and let the thing down, all eight tons of it. The little cuss had worked so hard his face was all red, but after that it was white as a sheet for the rest o' the day!"

Horses at Robinson Farm in Maple Corner.

Animal power was essential to maple sugarin' and for all walks of life in the early days of Vermont. As I have said, our ancestral farm was in Maple Corner, a small hamlet in the town of Calais. Maple Corner is eight miles north of Montpelier and served the hospitality needs of travelers going from Montpelier to Hardwick and points north back in the 1800s. It was a thriving little community with a general store, a stagecoach inn just down the road in Kents' Corner, and various mills powered by water. Traveling in those days required thought and planning, and the eight miles between Montpelier and Maple Corner produced lore of its own.

My father told of the stagecoach route that went from Montpelier through Maple Corner to Hardwick way back then. It came close to what is now the Morse Farm Maple Sugarworks, up the same hill that traffic now climbs so easily. There were two teams of rugged draft horses pulling out of Montpelier for the all-day trip to Hardwick. At the top of Clay Hill, just one mile north of Montpelier, they would stop at the first of many granite watering tubs. The next tub was located at a spring on the western side of the Morse Farm, where County Road used to be. At the reins on that route was one Truman Way. Truman was a colorful man, the

Kents' Tavern in the village of Kents' Corner.

Morse sugarhouse on Robinson Farm in Maple Corner. Same sugarhouse was moved and is now at Morse Farm Maple Sugarworks in East Montpelier.

Vermont version of a Wild West teamster. He wore a broad hat, ragged leather outerwear and spoke with a booming voice. His commands to the horses were loud and stern but he was good with the teams and he knew their limits. As the story goes, he announced himself as he approached every village or settlement: "I am the way, the only way, the TRUE WAY!"

My father also told of a man who "improved nature just a little" on the route to Maple Corner. His homestead lay at the edge of a swampy area, and County Road went close by that same swamp. Drainage was a real problem at certain times of the year. At those times, the old guy got up early in the morning and diverted water from the swamp onto the road. That extra bit of "slippage" proved just enough to bog down travelers. Of course, the old guy was happy to help them out—for a price!

Back then, animals worked as the "tractors" on the farm and each job required different levels of pulling power. Sometimes oxen were used in sugarin' instead of horses. Horses acted too high strung for the specialized job of sugarin' whereas oxen had the strength necessary to navigate huge depths of snow. They had a certain "plodding" nature that horses lacked and possessed a rather unique personality.

Sidney Morse, Road Commissioner, 3rd from left, poses with road crew and grader at No.10 Pond, Calais, Vermont, 1916.

After the market for eggs fell off back in the late fifties, we converted the chicken house to a loose housing barn for young stock. The critters were moved in at frost time to spend the winter there in the "pen barn." Yearlings were kept downstairs and the small calves, upstairs. As winter went on, the animals grew as did the manure and bedding under their feet. One spring morning, my brother Elliott went to the pen barn to do chores and found that the pen holding those young calves gave way during the night. The weight of the manure proved too much for a structure built for chickens and the calf pen floor dropped, calves and all, eight feet to the level below. There stood six happy calves, still standing on the manure-laden pen floor, chewing their cuds and acting as if nothing ever happened.

This laid back nature earned bovine oxen the "beast of choice" for many old time sugarmakers. Farmers used these pulling animals for field and woods, but also needed animals for power. Animal "power" was an early version of the modern day tread mill. An animal was enclosed on an endless belt placed on an incline.

Susie and Burr Morse communicating with 4-H calves, 1958.

Because of the incline, the animal naturally walked to avoid discomfort. This in turn powered a wide range of equipment from circular saws to grist mills. Horses were good "power" animals. I never heard of cattle being used for this purpose. My guess is that their level of intelligence did not lend itself to the job. Goats, on the other hand, were excellent animals in this capacity. And in these parts, when you think about goats, you think about Rome Van Ornem, who lived at the edge of Curtis Pond.

Rome was a crusty old bachelor from Maple Corner. His place was a menagerie of barnyard animals, but goats were his specialty. I grew up hearing stories about him and remember personally sitting in his ramshackled living room with my father and sister. Susie and I, seven and four, sat timidly on his tattered couch, legs dangling midair. Our father was there to discuss some farm matter. Rome had an old grandfather clock, its "tick-tock" made music with the bleating goats outside. A collection of stringed instruments lay around, dwarfed by the big upright piano; Rome was musical.

He "bitched and belly-ached," as my father put it, about all life's little challenges. That night, I remembered him complaining about his "darned hearing aid needing new batrys"—strange the things we remember. And the funny story he told that night remained etched in my memory.

He had been across the brook to his makeshift milking parlor and returned with two pails of goat milk. As he crossed the brook, a plank broke under his feet. In his nasally high pitch voice he said, "There I was flat on my back and couldn't get up. The pails tipped over and all my milk was spillin' down the brook. Then a gosh-darned billy goat came along and started suckin' on my ear!" Susie and I laughed and laughed at the thought of a billy goat doing that. With or without goats, Rome was a colorful character.

Life seems too easy these days. Today we hop in our car and make that trip from Maple Corner to Montpelier in ten minutes as compared to the hour to two hour horse ride of my ancestors. Our houses are heated with oil and we never worry about running out of food. Today's crises are more defined by high-speed accidents or terrorist attacks than being trampled by a horse or freezing to death. A return to the olden days, however, is not on my wish list. Those people had it hard, darned hard! They adapted to the circumstances, farmed and sugared in spite of contrary conditions. I appreciate the legacy they left behind. And I love this place, right down to my bones, and the nostalgia and history that comes with it. But no, I never want to turn back the hands of time and join them.

But we can and must remember as my son, Tom, does with this poem about his Grandfather, Harry, and the Calais Stage:

"Teazy," the goat at Morse Farm today.

The Calais Stage
By Tom Morse

Tom Morse, age 10,
with his uncle Elliott.

When I used to bring Harry for rides
I always knew the only direction to go was north,
Up the Calais Stage towards Maple Corner and Woodbury Gulf.
Before too long Harry would make his usual comment
About today's drivers with heavy feet and weak minds,
After all, Harry grew up in a time when the only traffic
On the road were a couple Model T's and the stage coach.

Harry's father, Sidney, drove the coach.
When the morning chores were done,
Young Harry would sometimes accompany his father,
And they would bring country folk down from the hills,
And into the village of Montpelier;
Then a day long trip, now a fifteen minute cruise,
For those with a heavy foot.

My Grandfather Harry and his father Sidney lived long lives,
Watched most of their road get paved,
And saw new houses sprout like clover,

In fields that no longer yielded hay.
While these changes saddened them,
They knew that change, like death and taxes was inevitable,
And welcomed in their new neighbors.

In his twilight years, when his driving days were over,
I had the privilege of taking Harry
On his beloved rides, up the old stage coach road,
Past his birthplace, and past Maple Corner,
Where the road turns to dirt, and on into the Gulf,
Where there are no houses, and County Road
Looks like the Calais Stage that it once was.

Piano in the parlor of Harry A. Morse and Ella Giddings. Pictures in background are of John Morse and Emeline Tucker, great-great grandparents of Burr.

Traditional Times

Each February found us more and more anxious for sugarin' to begin. The sugar roads had all been "broke" out but we controlled our urge to get into the sugarbush and tap our trees.

Tapping means drilling holes two inches deep into each tree. A tap hole is a wound and tap wounds are viable for only about five weeks before the healing begins. If we tap too early, they may dry up before the end of sugarin'— tap too late and we miss the first sap runs of the year.

Traditionally in Central Vermont, we waited until after Town Meeting Day, the first Tuesday in March, blizzard or no blizzard, to tap our sugarbush. Local politics came first with local issues often decided based on conversation alone.

Hale Bowen, from up in Sheffield, was eighty-seven and the most respected member of his community. Living that long in a God-forsaken place just deserved that kinda respect. One day in early March, Mr. Tom Mattoon asked Hale how he felt about the upcoming Town Meeting. "I'm goin' for them beans," he said. This surprised Tom. The Bean boys, Eugene Sr. and Eugene Jr., were horse loggers by trade. By stature, they were drinkers, late sleepers, and quite stupid (not necessarily in that order). Eugene and Eugene had been placed on the Town Meeting ballot for First Constable and Fence Viewer, respectively.

Tom figured if old Hale was supporting the Beans, maybe they had some hidden merits and should be considered by the voters of Sheffield. He started talking them up. Town Meeting came with the usual bickering, acknowledgments and everyone's favorite part, the potluck meal at noon. After the ballots had been counted, the Beans had won by a landslide. A few days later Tom ran into old Hale down at the store.

"You sure pushed those Bean boys ovah the edge at Town Meetin', Hale."

"What do you mean, young fella?" Hale asked, "I didn't vote for those cusses!"

"You didn't?" said Tom. "But you told me you were goin' for the Beans!"

"Yessah," Hale boomed. "Bertha Armstrong's baked beans is the only reason I've evah gone to Town Meetin'!"

The day after the Town Meeting of 1972, we headed for the sugarbush with all of our gear. We carried stacks of buckets, boxes of covers, and pails full of spouts on a sled pulled by the old bulldozer. Normally we would just be "scattering buckets" at this early point in the season, but on this day we decided to tap and hang them, too. Snow was forecasted and we pictured having to dig out all 3,000 buckets from under twelve inches of snow.

Four of us were working: My father, Harry, Gerald Pease, a boy sent up from the Department of Rehab, and me. We all wore snowshoes except for Gerald. I carried the tapping machine, a nasty little two-cycled engine with a drill bit the size of a small cigar. The thing wouldn't start so we tinkered on it, and we tinkered on it! We remembered the prior season and cursed ourselves for forgetting the problems with the tapper for the past eleven months. Finally the tinkering paid off, the thing started and we began tapping trees and hanging buckets.

Father carried a hammer and a carpenter's apron that bulged with spouts. Gerald moved the bulldozer (he called her Aunt Betsy) ahead and handed stacks of buckets and piles of covers to the boy. Covers were important to the maple process because they kept out rainwater and snow. We used two pitched covers, like little pup tents. They had grooves on each side that slid over a flange on top of the bucket, a system that withstood most windstorms.

First in line, I approached each tree with the caution of a naturalist, the

Gerald Pease and the boys, workin' with "Aunt Betsy."

anticipation of a sugarmaker, and the productivity of a businessman all wrapped in one. I found places to tap that were not too close to old tap holes, decided how many holes to drill so that we got optimum sap, and was sure that I didn't damage the tree.

Maples are wild trees; it takes a maple forty years to grow big enough to tap the first time. We wait that long because we can't risk damaging them. It's possible to over tap a tree.

Mr. Watson, over on Collar Hill, set out to do just that one year, tap a tree to death. He wanted to get rid of the tree, needed an additional source of firewood, and loved his maple syrup. He decided to run an experiment and find out how much tapping a maple would torerate. He drilled tap holes around the bottom of the tree, pounded spouts, and hung buckets. Next, he moved up a step and repeated the process. Before Watson finished, he worked from a ladder hanging buckets way up in the middle of that tree, fifty buckets in all. After three years of this abuse, the tree finally died and he ended up with a big woodpile and lots of nice fancy syrup. Vermont was a Republican state back in those days, but Watson voted Democrat. The scuttlebutt around Calais that year found Watson guilty, by conversational politics alone, of bleeding a maple tree to death!

(David Aiken Photo)

For three days we tapped, pounded spouts, hung buckets, and put on covers. It was hard labor by anyone's standards, but the job for this year was done and the waiting began, the wait for sap weather.

Sap will only run if it freezes at night, thaws during the day and the wind direction is right. Pretty fussy, you may say. Sugarmakers are more than fussy—we're downright neurotic! Nightly freezes are very necessary, but too much cold will freeze the sap into solid ice. Daily thaws are also necessary, but too much warmth will spoil the sap and encourage buds to swell. And the wrong wind direction brings the wrong atmospheric pressure, preventing the tree's inner pressure from pushing the sap out.

When the wind's from the North, sugarmakers go forth.
When the wind's from the East, the sap runs the least.
When the wind's from the South, the sap runs drought.
When the wind's from the West, the sap runs best.

In a way, good weather is bad for sugarmakers and bad weather is good for sugarmakers. Some years sap weather starts as we tap and tapping becomes a complete frenzy; other years it holds off until mid to late March. Those years all we can do is wait.

In 1972, winter's grip on us finally loosened on March 20. (The first sap day is always packed with excitement.) Thankfully our tapping crew that year survived intact and became the gathering crew. Gerald was a dairy farmer in the next town and gladly gathered sap between chores. The boy from the state caught on and a young man from Colorado with a dog and a big school bus appeared at the last moment.

Sugarmakers are innovators. Heavy, sloshing gathering buckets and deep snow begs creativity in the hauling of sap. Since sugarmakers gauge their needs on the number of trees they tap, equipment ranges from man-powered children's sleds to huge ones drawn by horses. Up in Vermont's Franklin County, the last vestige of traditional sap gathering, the conveyance of choice is a hardwood sled carrying a five barrel gathering tank pulled by a team of horses. Late into the season, the sled is replaced by a rubber-tired wagon constructed low to the ground and pulled by the same team. Many of these traditional sugarmakers are large dairy farmers and have several high horsepower tractors at their disposal. They refuse, however, to pull the gathering tank with a tractor. It tears up the land too much. For that simple reason they keep horses all year.

When gathering sap on the Morse Farm, we used a trailer with tandem truck tires, pulled by huge Aunt Betsy, the bulldozer. We were careful to not abuse the land with our heavy equipment. One particular day back then, we really appreciated the flotation of those big tires on the soft snow.

That year, a girl from Chicago helped with the sap gathering. A bunch of us made our way through the woods with old Aunt Betsy pulling our dual wheeled trailer. I was driving and suddenly realized the girl was missing. I stopped, got off,

(David Aiken Photo)

and walked back a ways. She had fallen off the trailer. There she was around the bend, pulling herself out of four feet of snow and examining two wheel marks imprinted on her mid-section. Thanks to the cushioning of the deep snow, she was okay. I had run over her without causing any harm. She was kind of pretty and I'm glad I didn't kill her on the first day out.

Gerald headed up the gathering crew in 1972. They washed eleven month's worth of cobwebs from the gathering tank's interior, Gerald found three sets of five-gallon gathering pails and they headed out for the sugarbush: Gerald, the young man from Colorado, and the boy from the state. Buckets were heavy with sap, some overflowed. It dripped fast and excitement of a good run buffered the grueling job of gathering.

Dad related a story about sending his hired man out to the sugarbush one day to check on how fast the sap was running. Old Bill was gone awhile and returned all excited. "By gory, I counted eighteen drops between the end-a-the spout and the bottom-a-the bucket!" he said. Dad said Bill "never amounted to a darn" in school, but ended up a wicked fast counter anyway!

Good sap 'runs' that fill up three-gallon buckets in eight hours are total exhilaration to a sugarmaker. Most folks have a hard time seeing this as excitement!

Gerald's crew filled the 500-gallon tank in about an hour that first day and headed back to the sugarhouse. Meanwhile my father and I washed the main storage tank and leveled the evaporator, getting ready to boil. While the sap was unloaded, the gathering crew went to the farm house and found a quick meal of corn chowder made with real cream.

Times have changed, culinary techniques and eating habits are no exception. We were dairy farmers. We made our living from the sale of milk and cream and used it, too. I guess we couldn't expect folks to support our industry if we didn't support it ourselves; plus, darn it all, whole milk, cream and butter just made food taste better! These days, people are paranoid of a little too much fat. They buy skim milk, margarine, and "fat free" everything. No wonder there's so many unhappy people. FAT IS FLAVOR.

My mother Dot Morse speaks of "slathering" this and that with butter and her cookin' is so good. I think we got by eating like that because we worked so hard. In defense of modern people and all their dieting, I believe they really can't eat like we did because they don't physically work as hard.

One time I was eating over at Gerald and Ellen Pease's place. We were haying and ravenously hungry. Ellen served zucchini that was wonderful. I mean, zucchini just does not taste that good. I asked her how she did it and she replied, "Oh, I just add a little hog fat!"

Fortified, the gathering crew headed back to the sugarbush for the second load. They gathered from 3,000 taps, and had close to 3,000 gallons of sap by day's end. Adrenaline really "kicked in" when buckets were full and running over. Camaraderie grew with the gathering crew. Gerald set the tone with his clipped "one liners"; he loved sugarin' and asserted himself as boss. He was good with the equipment and the two boys respected their place in his realm. Nature surrounded the gatherers on this sunny 45° day. Conditions were perfect for the millions of minute snow fleas that littered the snow and an occasional crow that interrupted the quiet. Some squirrels scuttered about while others provided surprises. Harry told of an aging hired man, of "Yankee persuasion" who gathered sap in our woods one time:

"He trudged along with his two gathering pails, stopping at every tree. He slid off the covers and carefully lifted the buckets from their spouts, poured the sap into his pails. He was careful with every drop of sap and made a slow and painstaking walk back to the gathering tank. At one tree he slid off the cover and there, floating in the sap, was a drowned squirrel." Harry continued with a devilish grin, *"Even a Scotch old Vermonter would, you know, throw it out—well, at least the squirrel!"*

Squeamish readers take note: that sap really would have been thrown out. We use plastic tubing these days, an "animal proof" system of gathering!

There was never a shortage of "characters" that showed up for sugarin'. My grandmother, Mildred Robinson Morse, told of an ancestor who was a little "slow," (she used the term "foolish"). His name was Mr. Drury Rich. In Mildred Morse's words:

"Drury Rich was living at the Calais poor farm back in the late 1800s. Poor farms in that day were for folks who were not productive in society. Drury was placed in the poor farm at a young age. One day, he came running in from the hayloft all out of breath—'Amassy Tucker is hanging by his neck

CURTIS POND, CALAIS, VT. 34.

Curtis Pond in Rome's time.

from a timber,' he reported. The overseer reacted with great alarm, asking Drury if he had cut Amassy down. Drury meekly replied: 'God, I didn't know if he was dead yet!'"

Sugarin' brings out some characters that are not too swift and characters that are almost too smart for their own good.

Not far from the Calais poor farm lived Rome Van Ornem, the town goat farmer. Goats are smart animals and maybe some of it rubbed off on Rome, but one time his intelligence backfired, literally.

Rome took two touring ladies for a boat ride on Curtis Pond one July day. He rowed slowly while telling the ladies facts about the area. After an hour in the boat he felt a spell of flatulence coming on. Being an independent old bachelor and quite used to letting nature have its way, he puzzled over how to handle the situation. At once, his trusty muzzleloader came to mind.

"Ladies, you see that biggest lily pad ovah theyah?" he asked. They acknowledged the lily pad.

"You wanta see me blow that lily pad outa the watah?" The two city ladies agreed, recognizing the "character" in Rome. He loaded up the gun, not a moment too soon as nature demanded proper timing. He aimed and pulled the trigger but the boat ride ended all wrong for Rome that day—the gun misfired!

Just up the road from Rome lived the Brown Family. One step ahead of the poor farm, they lived the only way they knew. Life was hard and sometimes not fair. Daughter Marion was born with a slow mind, perfect fuel for folk lore.

Marion lived with her father and two brothers up on Ellis Hill above Maple Corner during the mid-1800s. They were a resourceful, deep–rooted bunch, eating and clothing themselves off the land. Her father, old Lyman, was a big, fat man who acquired his stature by eating too much and working too little. He was too lazy to help with the hunting, trapping, and barn chores, but managed to get elected to the Vermont Legislature from Calais. The eight mile trip to Montpelier was difficult to make each day, so he took a room in town. There he settled into the good life like a pig to wallow.

One day, old Lyman died in the legislative dining room. Two men from the legislature traveled up County Road to Ellis Hill to inform his family of the death. Marion was home alone. Her brothers were out hunting.

"Marion," one of the men said. "I'm afraid we have some bad news to tell you."

"Bad neeews?"

"Yes, Marion, bad news. Your father died today at the legislature."

"Doyd?" she said in her deep, bass voice.

"Yes, Marion, he died."

"Is he deaaad?"

"Yes, he's dead."

"Gonna skin 'im?"

Maybe, Marion wasn't so slow after all. We all have a politician or two that we'd just as soon do that to!

If you've been to the Morse Farm Maple Sugarworks and had Sugar on Snow, you may recall meeting Audrey Lafirira. Audrey is the granddaughter of Harry Daniels. Harry Daniels was a bit "rough and tumble." He left no uncertainty about his thoughts, Parliamentary procedure or not.

Harry Daniels represented the town of Woodbury in the Vermont Legislature back in the late 1800s. He was a crusty old cuss who seldom spoke but when he did, he did so with curt shrewdness. One day the legislature was debating whether or not to rename Woodbury Pond, Mirror Lake. There was considerable debate and old Daniels remained silent through much of it. It reached a point, however, when the debate was striking too close to home and he rose suddenly.

"Mr. Speaker, I wish to address this noble body."

"You may proceed, Mr. Daniels," replied the Speaker.

"Mr. Speaker, as you know, I represent the town of Woodbury and this is a very familiar body of water to me. This body of water, Mr. Speaker, is small in area. This body of water, Mr. Speaker, is not a lake — it's too small. Why furthermore, Mr. Speaker, it's so small that I could pass water half way across it."

With this, the Speaker pounded down his gavel and boomed, "Mr. Daniels, you are out of order!"

Old Daniels thundered, "Mr. Speaker, I know very well I'm out of ordah. If I wasn't, I could pass water all the way across it!"

Regardless of the method used to gather that precious sap, the sugarin' season still brings out those colorful characters. There are many folks who still feel the best syrup is made by gathering sap from sap buckets, but there was a "time and place." Our "place" is the same but our "times" are changing; we entered a new era for maple sugarin' with the close of the 1974 season. ❧

Changing Times

Vermont's maple image is steeped in tradition. Like all other agricultural ventures, however, maple sugarin' has incorporated less labor-intensive ways of doing things out of necessity. We're now using plastic tubing to bring our sap to a central place and that means there's no more trudging through the deep snow and thick mud with heavy equipment and gathering crews. The modern sugarmaker trudges on toward a different but no less noble venture; making top quality syrup for a global market with an eye toward the bottom line.

On February 16, 1975, my father and I headed for the sugarbush armed with tubing, tools and accessories. This was our first experience with plastic tubing except for a cursory lesson from a neighboring sugarmaker. We decided to start with just 600 trees on a south facing hillside. We needed snowshoes.

One of the surviving bastions of traditional sugarin' is a pair of snowshoes. They are ageless and at day's end, downright evil, but as long as there's snow in Vermont in February and sugarin' to do, there will be snowshoes.

I never had snowshoe lessons. Father just took me aside one day and said: "Son, there are two easy steps to using these things. First, walk like a small boy who has just filled his pants. Second, use the bathroom before you get into 'em, cause it's hell to get out of 'em. He looked at me with a sparkle in his eye. Now you're an expert!"

Now, in late winter, I worked in the sugarbush on the plastic tubing. Though we sugarmakers view tubing as a great thing, it still requires lots of hard, sugarbush-trudging work.

Last year at this time I was "crowing" about a firm crust that we walked on, but every year is different for the sugarmaker. This year was a snowshoe year.

There is no set calendar date for the first appearance of snowshoes, unlike long underwear. I, in fact, avoid them like the plague until they are absolutely necessary. When the wallowing gets harder than wearing snowshoes, I strap 'em on.

We started using snowshoes in early January 1975, when the "wallow test" failed. Within each year, there are good snowshoe days and bad snowshoe days.

I thought about this book on bad snowshoe days; yesterday was one for sure. The temperature was in the mid–thirties and our snow was soft. I donned my trusty shoes (I still like the wooden ones lovingly maintained with duct tape and drywall screws), and headed out about 9:00 A.M. On a good snowshoe day, which usually coincides with cold temperatures, snowshoes don't sink in too much. Yesterday, however, those dreadful appliances dropped in a good ten inches and withdrew six pounds of sticky "terra flaka" with every step. Plodding was the word for the day!

The good thing about bad snowshoe days and plodding is that the plodder has plenty of time to think and ponder. Sometimes the thoughts get a little "funky." For a while I counted snow fleas, but that got too funky after 12,008. Then I imagined I saw Gnomes crouching behind trees. They laughed because the snow held them up just fine. But mostly, I mentally wrote out this book, chapter by chapter, story by story, while I plodded through the sugarbush preparing for the season.

Our understanding in 1975, and now, is that tubing is an artery system. Mainlines run up the valleys, or low points, and smaller tubing branches off to each individual tree. The main tenet of a tubing system is that water only flows downhill. We are farmers, not plumbers, but we understand that principle.

Luckily, the slope where we worked was ample, but we carried a sight level just in case. We trudged to the far end of that part of the sugarbush to start; wisdom begged we made our mistakes there. I attached the tubing to the last tree and my father slowly uncoiled tubing from the roll he carried as he headed downhill. He selected a zigzag route around trees and headed toward the mainline. Finally, we stretched it like a rubber band. Our early days of tubing lacked any real planning. We flew by the seat of our pants. My father mused over a "Chaplinesque" scenario: the uncoiling process was fast-forwarded and when we stretched the tubing, it disconnected at a fitting and the stretcher fell head over heels.

Following that first tubing adventure, it took three years to adapt all 3,000 of our maple trees to the system. We designed our tubing to stay in place all year long, but were told that there were folks who take it down for storage after every season. That sounded impossible to us. Being permanent, however, made it subject to natural wear and tear. With our completed tubing system, the last days of February were spent patrolling the lines and fixing all of the last year's damage.

This work can't be done with gloves. After an hour, even with that protection, our hands felt like they would shatter like glass, but we couldn't stop.

If the system was left sagging or with squirrel holes, any gains over the bucket system was lost.

Squirrels are a problem for the modern sugarmaker. They chew tubing! They may attack it at every tree, chew randomly or even take the plastic spouts home for storage. It is now quite common for loggers to find caches of spouts in the squirrel dens of large maples.

One day I reached the height of my frustration with squirrels. Shouldering the shotgun, I headed for the sugarbush. Having a million other things to do, I hurried along, hoping trees would be full of the rascals. As luck would have it, they were not, and I soon headed home. Somewhere deep in the South End, my eyes beheld a sudden "whoosh," followed by a dull "plop" at my feet. I looked down and there lay the biggest, deadest, old gray squirrel I had ever seen. I wondered: "Is this a Divine message that my squirrel problem will be solved, just a cruel prank by Mother Nature, or simple coincidence?" At any rate, my walk in the sugarbush netted one less squirrel that day.

With proper maintenance and an annual investment of labor, tubing can be a great boon to maple sugaring. Back when plastic tubing was first introduced, we sugarmakers were Guinea pigs for the plastics manufacturers. Because sugarin' is a small industry, globally speaking, there has always been a shortage of research money, so on-the-job research was the norm. In our first tubing attempts, we made multiple mistakes, which in many cases necessitated rebuilding the tubing systems too quickly, or in extreme cases, returning to buckets.

One of our local sugarmakers, Preston Baker, was getting on in age. Sugarin' was more difficult for him with every passing year. Folks told him to convert to this new plastic tubing—said it would save all sorts of time and make his life easier. He finally relented and spent all winter nearly freezing to death installing the tubing. Although he did the best job he could, much of it was poorly done. Sugarin' for him that year only delivered a third of a crop of sap. Some flowed out squirrel holes onto the ground. And some stayed right in the trees because the tubing was installed uphill instead of down. After the season, he took it down and threw it away—said he'd die gathering from buckets before he'd try the stuff again. By God he did, too—dropped right in his tracks the next season. Spilt two gathering pails of good sap when he keeled over!

Tubing technology has improved greatly over the last twenty years. We've found that washing our tubing systems with a Clorox solution aggravated our squirrel problem. Clorox leaves a salt residue which just attracts them. We now clean our tubing with pure Vermont water. There are new ways of fastening tubing to trees that are much kinder and gentler than nailing and we apply vacuum to the systems for extraction. This sometimes circumvents the weather conditions and allows sap to run when nature is not quite cooperating. It's commonly accepted that this does not harm the trees, but instead may actually help them. Multiple tap wounds are what harm maple trees and a vacuum allows us to tap more conservatively.

Folks ask us if we are glad we went modern in the sugarbush. That is a hard question. We, at Morse Farm, never did give up on tubing (like Preston Baker), even though our tubing experience had been equally traumatic. Today we are comfortable with our new system. Those years of experience, advances in the industry, and hiring a guy named David Sparrow helped a lot.

A few years ago, I needed to replace a hired man who had just quit. The job required a special person, one who was good with equipment and would work both indoors and outdoors; in short, the perfect job for an ex-dairy farmer. The person I found was David Sparrow, who had not found any job he really liked since the family dairy herd had been sold. He agreed to accept my offer on a trial basis. David had been on the job a short while when I realized he was perfect for our place. At that time, we were getting very frustrated with plastic tubing and the slow pace of our modernization. David's solutions were simple and based on his dairy background. He was wise with the workings of vacuum pumps, bucket loaders and chuck wagons, all things that we put to work under his tutelage.

Now most of our maple sap is being gathered by a well-tuned, "David Sparrow" vacuum system. A wood chip gasifier, another of David's installations, boils our sap and a used dairy chuck wagon, modified by David, automates the wood chip handling.

At long last, our progression to modern day sugarmaking is complete. We have made every mistake in the book, sometimes measuring progress in inches rather than miles. We have researched, experimented, capitalized and amortized and, yes, we have lost some of the romance. No longer do woolen-clad men drive horses from tree to tree, gathering sap with pure muscle and grit. And in some sugarhouses, the crackling of the fire has been replaced by the blast of an oil burner. But these changes are insuring the future of our industry. Technology, driven by economics, has brought sugarin' to a new level. 🍁

Boiling: That Great First Day

Back at the sugarhouse, Harry touched a match to the first fire of the season. Maple sap is boiled down to maple syrup in an evaporator and the part of the evaporator that holds the fire that provides the necessary heat is called the arch. The arch is first laid with ample kindling to start the dry, hardwood fire. Fuel for a wood fired evaporator is called "sugar wood" and may be hard wood, soft wood or a mixture. The best syrup is made with very rapid boiling, so the flashiness of the fire is important.

On this day, the draft was extra strong and Harry's fire took off with a soft groan. Crackling sounds of a wood fire and little "pops" of expanding metal filled the sugarhouse. Within fifteen minutes, steam started to rise from the open front pan followed by the rumbling of a rolling boil in the back pan. That first whiff of "new syrup" brought the excitement to a peak and marked the real beginning of this new season. All the labor that came before was just work that had to be done.

Another of nature's sugarin' secrets is the sweetness of sap. We have sweet years and watery years, but on average, sap is only two percent sugar. At that sweetness, it takes about forty gallons of sap to boil down into one gallon of pure maple syrup. We always hope for a sweet year when this ratio can be as good as twenty-five gallons to one, but only a foolish sugarmaker plans on that. Sugarmakers never know when Murphy's Law will step in and take the course of sugarin' in another direction. That ratio may be as bad as ninety to one. Harry told of one sweet year, followed by a terrible one:

"One year back in the early seventies we had one of those sweet years. Sap was hovering around twenty-five to one and, oh boy, was it runnin'! At that sweetness, it boils fast and uses much less fuel. The faster sap boils, the lighter in color the syrup will be. We were making all super fancy syrup that year, and it just wouldn't quit at 5:00 P.M., you know. We'd boil 'til midnight, one, two, or three in the morning, and still have sap in storage. Under those circumstances, you're dog tired and sick of being on your feet, but you know it's going to run like hell tomorrow and you're not going to let it run on the ground. My son, Burr and I took turns boilin' around the clock and finally Paul Cate and one of his friends from forestry school came along

and offered to boil. They were good smart kids, so we let them take over during the night. Between the four of us, we kept that old sugarhouse a humpin' for a week steady before the run slowed down.

We sugarmakers think of fancy syrup as the best, 'cause it is made at the beginning of the season when the weather is cool and the sap keeps best. For most city folks, however, it is too delicate in flavor and they don't like it so well. We had trouble selling all our fancy that year!

The next year was just the opposite. It took sixty gallons to make one that year and the season ended suddenly after a warm spell. Sugarin' lasted only two weeks that year— warm weather starts the buds to swell and gives the syrup a bitter, buddy flavor. Warm weather also spoils the sap so it'll only make dark syrup. We made a short crop that year, didn't have hardly any fancy. You never know what a sugar season'll be like! Folks ask me every year in February how good a season I'm expecting. I say, come back and ask me in May!"

This year Harry did the boiling, careful to maintain a boiling depth of just one inch. He watched to make sure the flow of sap into the evaporator was steady.

The back pan of an evaporator is the flue pan, a heat exchanger designed to receive the sap first and boil it extra quickly. Since the flow of raw sap is constantly entering the flue pan, it displaces what is already there and pushes it through into the front pan. Sweeter and a bit heavier because of all the flue pan's boiling, the sap is then forced to travel through the front pan's channels, boiling the whole way. As it travels along, it gets sweeter and sweeter.

Harry Morse and Kenneth Fowler cut sugarwood with an early "two man" chainsaw.

One summer day I was in our sugarhouse telling folks how the evaporator worked. When I got to the front pan, I explained how the sap traveled along, getting sweeter and sweeter as it went. I slowed for effect and equated it to how my wife, Betsy, gets sweeter and sweeter as she goes along, too. The folks thought that was funny, except for one guy. He allowed as how his marriage was more like the flue pan—hotter than hell with little substance! I knew the guy had an attitude when I reached the end of my spiel and he said, "I don't like it here in

"Bucking" a log with an early two man chainsaw.

Vermont. You don't have no billboards!"

One reason maple sugarin' is so unique is that it is so short-lived. The sugarhouse bustles with activity for one month each year and then sits around collecting cobwebs the other eleven! Evaporators are a specialized piece of equipment, made only for concentrating maple sap. After that job is done, they are cleaned, blocked up for proper aeration, and left as expensive props for the cobwebs. It takes real creativity to figure out any off-season use for an evaporator.

Old Augustus Aldrich figured it out, however. One August day Harry Morse and his cousin, Sam Kent, traveled to the southern Vermont town of Weathersfield to visit Old Gus. Gus was a maker of apple cider jelly, a product that can be boiled in the front pan of a traditional maple sugarin' evaporator. We were thinking of doing just that back at our sugarhouse for our new mail order company. Gus was the only person doing it at the time and willing to share his secrets.

Harry and Sam arrived at Gus' sugarhouse to a welcoming dog and a mish-mash of tools and machinery scattered about. Clean, white steam spewed from the cupola, a fragrant enigma for that time of year. They got out of their car, passed the dog's inspection, and headed for the sagging doorway. Entering, they witnessed a sight forever etched in their memories. Harry observed: "There stood Gus Aldrich, stooped over the old copper front pan, hands gloved and lowered, obviously pushing something along."

Upon closer inspection, they found the object he held was an old, retired pair of overalls. Harry continued "They were down in the boilin' cider. He used them to chase the cider along from one compartment to another. Sam started singin', 'Who Put the Overalls in Mrs. Murphy's Chowder?' much to my embarrassment. It didn't seem to bother old Gus! He was intent on his duties and only welcomed us when the batch of jelly was finally pushed to the draw-off valve."

Gus was in his mid-eighties.

"He explained the process to us, including tricks that most folks would have kept secret, like the makeup of the front pan. He said it must be copper, so the metal won't react with the acidity of the cider, and he went on to tell us just where he got that copper pan. With a twinkle in his eye, he said it would last him another fifteen years and he knew where he could get another one just like it, when it gave up. We thought that was so funny. Gus lived another twelve years after that and when he went, it was while hiking alone on Mount Katahdin in Maine. They never found him. And he never did tell us where that other copper front pan was!"

After about two hours of boiling, the sweet stuff in the final compartment of the front pan assumed a "blobby" look. Harry knew what syrup looked like when it was ready. He scooped into it with a flat edged dipper and let it pour off, back into the front pan. It "sheets" off the dipper's flat edge—the syrup was ready to draw off. He filled a deep metal cup up with the liquid and lowered a hydrometer into it. Syrup must weigh eleven pounds to the gallon. This exact density was critical because under-boiled syrup ferments and over-boiled syrup crystallizes. He cracked open the gate valve and allowed a stream of syrup to drain into a pail.

Syrup boils at seven degrees above the boiling point of water or about 219°F when it is ready.

Harry was very cautious of the evaporator level while drawing off finished syrup. Boiling syrup scorches easily and stories abound of sugarmakers who get distracted for one reason or another.

Bob Eastman entrusted his hired man with the boilin' one night. It was the middle of a big run and Bob was tired. Sometime around midnight, the hired man got into the sauce. One beer led to another and he ended up quite drunk. He fell asleep in his chair.

When Bob came back in the morning that front pan was fried! Melted solder and molten syrup mixed over what remained of the fire. God it stunk! The man was just beginning to stir and Bob kicked his butt outa there—said it was lucky the whole sugarhouse didn't catch. Bob was done sugarin' forever. It would have cost too much to replace that rig. They used the sugarhouse after that as a calf barn. Guess that place was just meant to stink!

Harry drew off a big batch of five gallons. At the end, the hydrometer showed too high a density in the pail. He opened the valve and allowed just enough under-boiled syrup in to equalize the density and then carried the pail of hot syrup over to the filtering table. He strained under the weight of his pail of syrup. With great care, he lifted the pail above three felt filter hats and slowly poured it in.

Syrup contains an impurity called niter, a sandy mineral substance from the trees. If left unfiltered, it will detract from the flavor.

In his tongue-in-cheek style, Harry told of a bad niter experience:

> *"Niter looks good, much like peanut butter. A bunch of kids*
> *came in the sugarhouse one day and started running their*

fingers along the inside of the filter and eating that niter. It tastes good going down, but niter is an abrasive and it raises havoc with a person's digestive tract. Those kids were soon headed for the woods. They stayed away from the niter after that!"

The first boiling can bring surprises in grade. Usually, the first syrup made is a very light color with a delicate flavor. However, we sugarmakers are always nervous until we test it to make sure.

Harry drew a small amount of the new syrup into a pitcher as soon as it cleared the filter. He lifted the cover off a special wooden holder that contained four small bottles of different colored syrup and one empty bottle. The four colored bottles were not actually maple syrup, but colored glycerin, prepared by the State of Vermont. Each color represented the State's requirement for the four grades of syrup: Fancy, Grade A Medium Amber, Grade A Dark Amber, and Grade B. Harry filled the empty bottle with his new syrup, slipped it into the wooden holder and held it up to the light. The smile on his face said it all. Fancy, par for the course on the first day of boiling. He slipped it out of the holder, tipped it up to his lips and tasted it. His face beamed with the satisfaction only a Vermont sugarmaker knows. 🍁

The Greatness of Maple

I t is probably impossible for one man's words to reasonably portray the magic and ambience of maple sugarin'. For the true effect, one needs to be there, feeling the steam and inhaling that heavenly aroma. The real maple experience is felt best via personal osmosis, but for those under a geographical restraint, words must somehow suffice. Sugarin' deserves all the best words and the finest skill in putting them together, but Vermont sugarin' rates words of an even higher level. The word 'great' naturally comes to mind.

Vermont maple syrup has several personalities. The inability to recognize this would be like serving a five-course meal and calling it just 'soup' on the menu. We have a syrup grading law that has been on the books for ages. Vermont's grading law recognizes the personality of maple syrup with an eye toward helping the consumer. As you know, light-colored syrup is made at the beginning of the season when the weather is cool and the sap keeps better. The chemical nature of maple sap affects the flavor and color of the finished pure product. Sap's small amount of sugar is just enough to render the product unstable. Sugar sours and temperature affects the rate of that change. Our sugar season starts with cool weather and ends with warm weather, so naturally we boil different qualities of sap throughout the season. This would be best explained by another fellow Vermont sugarmaker:

Sample bottles of different grades of syrup at Morse Farm Sugarhouse.

"I'm a maple sugarmaker and I like fancy syrup, point blank. When I work at the maple booth at the fair every year, though, I give samples to lots a' folks. It's amazing how many of them say they prefer the darker grades. That's okay. In fact, that's great, as we need a market for all grades. You know, by the book (or Vermont sugarmaker), dark syrup grades are lower in quality, but if folks like them better, then it's high quality to them. We're just darned lucky to have the grading law so folks know what they're getting. There is one grade we don't normally include in the taste samples: Grade C or Frog Run. Frog Run's made the last days of the season when the frost is gone and the frogs are singin'. Usually by this time, the buds are swelling and that can give the syrup a buddy, bitter flavor.

You can't buy Grade C in a retail container because the State of Vermont doesn't want anyone turned off by the bitter taste, should it have one (not all Grade C is bitter). Grade C is sold in large bulk containers for the purpose of flavoring and blending. If you buy a nationally sold product (Heaven forbid!) with 'pure and artificial maple flavor' on the list of ingredients, you can be assured that the pure part of that is Grade C. But each to his own."

Clear as, well, Frog Run maple syrup, you say? The fact is, if it says "pure maple syrup" on the container and has a grade label, you can trust it. There is a real psychology to the perception of the syrup grades. We sugarmakers love the light syrup. It is, indeed, made from the best sap, collected early in the season. At that point, we are excited about sugarin'. The grade we make when we are excited is our favorite. Non-sugarmakers, however, know nothing about the special bouquet of light syrup or the excitement of early season. Many of them think syrup is supposed to be dark and robust. Some get downright suspicious about syrup that is light and delicate.

A guy came into our sugarhouse one day and wanted us to send a quart of our best to his father in Florida. We sent fancy, cause by the book, that is our best. When the old man in Florida got his syrup, he was mad! He sent us a letter calling us criminals, said we had adulterated the syrup. "This stuff is light and thin and weak. It is not nice and dark and robust like the real Log Cabin I'm used to!" What he meant, of course, was that fancy is too light and delicate for him. We sent him Dark Amber, and he loved it.

We Vermonters are proud, in fact downright righteous, about our maple syrup's great quality and pure image. We enjoy our mixture of farm and wilderness and have somehow kept development at bay; development that has both benefited and plagued our neighbors to the south and west. Our plague keeps a low profile, well camouflaged to the outsider by the beauty of the countryside, but to the Vermonter, it is darkly looming; we continue to lose our farms. Vermont has no

(Jackie Tollmann Photo)

ocean and our warm season is short, two qualities that may repel tourists. That compels us to be creative and recognize our proven assets. Vermont's maple image is one of our proven assets. We stand under a large magnifying glass with the world peering through, a world that sees a tiny American state with a big maple image. It is our maple syrup that brings people to Vermont and our natural beauty that keeps them here. Maple is great indeed! 🍁

The Morse Farm Today

With an earthy declaration that he "would rather milk people than cows," Harry Morse sold his dairy cows in 1966. He never looked back. Some time before that he had approached me, youngest of the litter, and asked me to be part of a new and different farming operation. I begrudgingly accepted at age seventeen. Actually, I had things I wanted to do with my life and bein' a farmer wasn't top on my list. In fact it wasn't on my list at all! I wanted to be a long distance truck driver or a music teacher or a writer, but never a farmer! I'm afraid I didn't always have the best attitude about the life he chose for me, but I've stayed on out of loyalty and now that I am getting old myself, you know, I like it! Yes I do, I love it here, and I have a feeling Dad's spirit probably knows that.

Harry Morse's dream was to keep the farm without milking cows and focus on his lifelong love of sugarin'—no easy matter in Vermont where dairy farming reigns as the only practical farming. To the ever-optimistic Harry, however, raising vegetables and beef cows seemed a reasonable complement to spring time sugarin'. With the support of Dot (his wife, life partner, and kindred spirit) and me, he built a sixteen by twenty foot vegetable stand and kicked off the new venture, ready or not.

Main entrance to Morse Farm Maple Sugarworks today, enhanced by Betsy Morse's morning glories.

We worked seven days a week, prodded on by persistence, Harry's dream, and most importantly, Dot's teaching salary. Occasionally, Harry would break from the fields and go to Montpelier's State Street, down by the Vermont State House. There he would pick out a tour bus, approach the escort, and suggest the whole group come up to the Morse Farm. Marketer extraordinaire, yankee entrepreneur, and visionary, Harry's dreams began to take form. Buses of tourists started coming to Morse Farm, and they came, and they came.

"I'd go down to the statehouse and promise these folks the world, if they'd come up to the sugarhouse. Some would look at me like I was a panhandler, but some would size me up as okay, and the bus would follow me right up the hill. The first group I got up here was Capital Tours from Springfield, Illinois. I just loved the folks on that bus and to make it especially worth their time, I laid it on a little thick. I'd throw in lotsa local color and make 'em laugh, but tell 'em about sugarin' at the same time. When I got done, they'd clap and whistle. It kinda made me feel good! I guess they really did like it 'cause Capital Tours kept coming back on their own and talked it up to other buses, too. Before long, we had lots of buses in the yard."

Today over 450 tour buses, scores of motor homes and private cars climb the hill from Montpelier to Morse Farm Maple Sugarworks each year. Harry passed away in 1999 and his legacy lives on—but it wasn't an easy act to follow.

Taking over my father's role as tour guide, jokester and most visible Vermonter at Morse Farm, was no easy matter. It happened all too suddenly with the onset of his fourth and harshest stroke. My first attempts were met with everything from guarded politeness to chilly catcalls, and I gained an instant respect for Dad's charisma. I tried using his material, his tone of voice, his dialect, but everything failed. My most monumental bomb happened the day I used his "milking" line which Harry could relate with seasoned charm.

"It was the year 1966, when I decided to stop milking cows. I didn't like the smell of the barn and my wife didn't like the smell of me when I came home from the barn. I decided to sell the herd and try my hand at milking people!"

Delivered by my Dad, that line always brought down the house, but when I tried it—no way! I learned what not to say in my fledgling season and, in a pleasantly surprising way, found that I had my own inherent humor.

One day I was explaining the magic of sugarin' to my audience. Being a seventh generation Vermont sugarmaker, few can do this better. I got to the slide in our show which pictures a drop of sap suspended between the end of the spout and the bottom of the bucket. I explained that sap never actually "runs," but always "drips," one drop at a time. During a good old-fashioned sap run the frequency of the dripping is fast enough to fill a three-gallon bucket in eight hours. "Wow!" I said, "That's a good, exciting run!" At once, the group erupted in laughter at my unintentional joke. To tourists, folks unfamiliar with the sugaring process, the thought of a sap bucket taking eight hours to fill up and being excited about it was hilarious. To a Vermont sugarmaker, it is exciting. I chuckled with them, kind of by default, and suddenly knew I COULD DO IT! From that day on, I milked that line with my best Vermont accent.

Now with my father gone, I am the tour guide, jokester, and most visible Vermonter in the Morse sugarhouse. I can't fill his shoes—I have to wear my own.

One thing we've never lost track of here at Morse Farm is the need to adapt to the times, production-wise and otherwise. A few years ago, we added wood sculptures to our attraction. Competition has grown over the last twenty years in the roadside sugarhouse business, and we had to adapt and update in order to 'stay ahead of the pack.' A few years ago, I went to the woods with my chainsaw to see if I had any eye as a sculptor. Much to my surprise, I did—I walked back that day with the face and torso of my Grandfather. I called him "Great Scott" because that was one of his favorite expressions. He was the first of many human characters I sculpted. These characters, along with Scott, include my great-great-great-uncle Aaron Tucker, my great-grandmother Nellie Robinson, Bill Gates (not the famous one, but a tobacco chewing, ex-hired man on the Morse Farm), and an Indian. They 'man' the antique farm equipment and tool displays at the Morse Farm.

"Great Scott," Burr's first sculpture.

Each has signage, tying him or her to lineage within the Morse family, to sugarin', or to the general area.

The most satisfying sculpting I have done is more freestyle than traditional chain saw sculpture. I find trees that already look like something and require only a minimum of sculpting. The first of these was from a yellow birch that grew within 100 feet of my house.

Sculpted spoofs on politics at Morse Farm.

I walked past it every day for twenty years on my way to work. One day, however, the right side of my brain must have been extra alert because there in that old yellow birch was an elephant! Just as plain as day, the ears drooped down both sides of a long trunk. All I needed to do was cut the tree down (which I did at considerable risk from high up in the bucket loader of our tractor) and carve a couple of eyes into the already formed face. It only took about thirty minutes to finish the elephant's face. Most of it was already made by nature.

Soon, I started stumbling across more of these forest creatures for my gallery. Since I had an elephant, I thought it would be fitting to have a donkey for the Democrats—a sugarhouse spoof on politics. I don't know if I was looking specifically for a donkey or not, but by God, I found one! There was a scrub apple tree and a black cherry tree growing together. They grew tangled around each other, almost as if they shared the same stump. I suspected that if I cut them down, inverted them, and added a tail, they would look like the posterior of a barnyard animal. For ten years now, the elephant's face has stood proudly beside the donkey's butt in our sugarhouse. There have been thousands of pictures taken of them. I tell folks, "This doesn't necessarily reflect my politics. I didn't tell those trees how to grow!"

Sometime after that I found Venus de Maple. Venus was part of a maple tree growing out of a ledge on the farm. Because of the ledge, the tree had been forced to grow horizontally for about three feet before it turned skyward. This tree held a unique peculiarity; the portion that was horizontal perfectly formed the legs and curves of a seated woman from the waist down. My task was to figure out what to add for the top half. I knew I wasn't talented enough to carve a face good looking enough to complete the level of feminine excellence that nature had provided for the bottom. A leverwood tree from my woods' travels came to mind. I remembered it as an unusual piece of wood with kind of a 'personality of its own' and was amazed upon my return visit; it had all the bumps in just the right places for the top half of a woman, minus the face. For some reason, the image of Venus de Milo suddenly came to mind, and as they say, the rest is history. I cut the leverwood tree down, and took the piece that I needed home, using the rest of the tree for sugar wood. I attached the piece to the maple bottom with plastic wood and named it Venus de Maple, knowing with a name like that, we could live with missing appendages like a head or arms! Folks sure do get a real kick out of Venus de Maple.

Ironically, most of the interest in Vermont sugarin' is at the time of year when we're not doing it. Vermonters come to the sugarhouse in the spring when we're boiling, but tourists are generally scared of our spring weather. Tourists trickle in

Burr's "Picassoesque" sculpture named "Pic Cow So."

during summer and flood in during our famous, but short-lived foliage season. In 2001, my older brother, Elliott, retired from being an auto mechanic and started working part time at the Morse Farm. Elliott has that old Vermont 'twang':

"While still workin' at the garage, I ended up in the hospital in the spring of 2001—had trouble with my breathin'—couldn't walk far at all. Bein' an EMT (Emergency Medical Technician), I knew what was wrong and knew better, but I ignored it for a while. I hoped it would go away. It didn't. I went in and they had me on the table within hours. They almost gave up on that balloon business, but finally one of the doctors busted through. They put one of those stents, like Cheney has, in the artery and sent me home. I was feeling almost Vice Presidential, when a week later my gut started to bother me. By God, I went back in and they found a blockage that required openin' me up. That time, I almost died. You know, when I finally did get out a' there, I said I'd never go back into that garage, and I never have.

I've been goin' over to the Morse Farm for a couple of years and helpin' with the tours. Don't tell Burr, but I talk better'n he does! I get on the buses and welcome folks and

then lead 'em into the sugarhouse where Burr usually takes
over. We make a good team and I love sugarin'. I tell folks
that sugarin's a disease and I've got it. I can't help it, and
I can't get rid of it! Our dad is proud of us; I just know that
he sees what's goin' on here."

Sugarin' continues at the Morse Farm much as it always has. We tap 3,000 trees every year and boil the sap in the same sugarhouse that Grandfather Sidney Morse moved fifty-two years ago from the ancestral farm in Maple Corner. Ten years ago, we installed a wood chip gasifier. A friend had finally talked me into woodchips saying they were real clean-burning and more economical than fuel oil. Wood chips are an automatic fuel so much easier to deal with than the traditional sugar wood. It's funny how fate steps in just in the nick of time.

That same year, I did a darn fool thing and went skiing over at one of the ski mountains. Fourth time down the mountain I lost control and scooted down over a bank and into a tree. Two things about a broken back; it hurts, and you have to stop working while it heals. While I sat around in a body cast, I thought about the upcoming sugar season. It would have been impossible for me to handle sugar-wood and I was glad we had installed the wood chip gasifier in the sugarhouse. Because of those woodchips, I was able to sugar that year even with a broken back.

With conversion to woodchips, we no longer needed the woodshed for storage of sugarwood. It occurred to me that a minimum of retrofitting would convert the

Woodshed Theatre at Morse Farm today.

woodshed into a theater. We stacked up some neat sugarwood walls, complete with an arched doorway, and put rows of stumps in for people to sit on. Morse Farm visitors now go to the famous Morse Farm Woodshed Theatre to view Harry Morse's humorous seventeen minute video. The video shows Harry telling a group from a tour bus about the maple process, complete with his trademark cuss words and witty one-liners. We hear hundreds of comments from visitors about "being sent to the woodshed."

Harry Morse did a sugarin' interview one time with a *Boston Globe* reporter. The man, an obvious greenhorn, simply wasn't warming up to Harry's clipped answers. He seemed bent on pinpointing maple science from start to finish and phrases like "b'guess and b'gory" didn't cut the mustard with him. We were in the middle of one of those hellish sap runs, and Harry was drawing off syrup like mad. The reporter was right in Harry's face with questions over density on the Brix scale and temperature in Celsius. Harry occasionally brushed him back from the evaporator, "Watch out, the darn stuff is hot." The interview was going sour, like sap on a hot day, when Gerald Pease walked in the sugarhouse. Now if anyone's more frugal with words than Harry Morse, it's Gerald Pease. Harry saw his chance to be free of the pesky reporter and introduced the two.

"So Mr. Pease," the reporter asked, "You been living around here all your life?"

"Not yet."

The reporter chuckled politely, "Now I'll assume you are a hardened Vermont expert in maple sugaring. Would that be an accurate assessment?"

"Got two chances," Gerald beamed.

"Just what do you mean, 'got two chances?'"

"I either is or I ain't."

With this, the *Boston Globe* reporter sensed the futility in the whole process and returned to Harry with one final question.

"Harry, I see you here making a lot of syrup and you have assured me of the quality. I assume that means it will be a good year."

With the wisdom only someone familiar with the quirks and surprises of a Vermont sugar season could muster, Harry replied, "Ask me in May, when the season's over."

The reporter left that day less than thrilled with Vermont effervescence. When the story finally came out, it contained lots of mistakes. Harry and Gerald guffawed as they read it. Gerald summed it up with his trademark, "Ha, Ha, Ha–how 'bout that!"

In recent months, Morse Farm was very fortunate gaining some national attention. Thanks to a lot of friends, we've had some exposure on national TV and in national magazines along with the local papers.

I was busy sugarin'. It hadn't been a great season so far, but even a mediocre sugar season was busy for us. One day early on, a *Burlington Free Press* photographer showed up in our sugarbush and photographed me stringing plastic tubing from tree to tree. He had been to the legislature down the hill and seemed quite delighted with the fresh air and change of pace the sugarbush offered. He fol-

Filming at Morse Farm.
(Larry Perry Photo)

lowed me for the longest time, click, click, clicking, bent on getting just the right shot. The next day I was featured on the front page of the *Burlington Free Press*, arms around a mid-sized maple tree in an apparent "forest love affair." The caption was "Tree Hugger" and it went out on the AP (Associated Press) to points all around the country.

Vermont sugarmakers do enjoy the limelight. Maple sugaring only occurs in a small portion of North America and receives worldwide attention because of its uniqueness. This year, Morse Farm Maple Sugarworks received its fair share of that attention. Our Maple Creemee (soft ice cream flavored with our own syrup) was featured in the March issue of *Food and Wine Magazine* on its list of "75 Best Food Buys in America." We were all so proud to be featured in that national venue.

Last year a crew from *Good Morning America* stopped at the Morse Farm and filmed me teaching a pretty correspondent named Lara, how to tap a maple tree. On the way to the tree, Lara fell into the soft snow. I was naturally glad to help her up. That same year *The Food Network* filmed a segment at Morse Farm for the Al Roker show. Wow! They were interested in all our maple things, especially our Maple Kettle Corn. I recall one "media" story from my younger years:

One day when I was attending fourth grade at the Morse School (yes, that was my school's name and my teacher's name was Mrs. Morse, my mother), my buddy Claude came in all excited: "Mrs. Morse," he exclaimed. "In the newspaper, Governor Keyser says sour grapes cause heart attacks!" When she pressed Claude for proof of this curious pronouncement, he produced from his pocket a rumpled clipping. It was headlined: "Gov. Keyser says, 'sour grapes to Hart attack.'" Claude crossed two politicians with an important medical breakthrough!

Harry would be proud of our changes and knowing that his grandson, Tom, has recently joined Morse Farm as a full-time employee. Today, twenty-five kilometers of well groomed ski trails wind around Morse Farm where the cows used to roam. Morse Farm vegetation today is measured more by aesthetics than by bushels, but that's okay—hills and valleys are still the same and those same old maples wait for their annual rite. Things go full circle. Sugarin' is a study in cycles; there are good years and bad years. We have had more than our share of bad years, lately, with maple decline, insect problems, and an ice storm of biblical proportions. Scientists hint of major problems like acid rain and global warming, ample fuel for the sugarin' pessimist. Our maples look healthy here right now and the sugarin' optimist disclaims dire projections. Last season was a bumper maple syrup crop and outside on this January day, the air is still and frigid. We wait. We wonder. Is the cycle swinging back? What secrets do those maples hold? Remember to ask us in May. 🍁

Of Bullwinkle and Bambi

Yesterday, I witnessed the striking personalities of two different critters out in the sugarbush. The day was warm and sunny. We were in the woods cleaning the tubing lines hung in cobweb-like networks from tree to tree. This was the final step toward closing the book on Sugarin' Season 2003. We found several places where the tubing had been pulled apart. This usually meant a limb had fallen and knocked the lines down. Our minds were somewhat baffled by the absence of fallen limbs, however, and completely baffled by one place where a portion of the woods stood barren of tubing. From one side of the gaping hole, a prostrate tubing line departed for the hinterlands. This suggested the probability that something large, like a bulldozer, had blundered into the line, pulled it from the trees, and dragged it away. We had followed the prostrate line part way to the hinterlands before we found telltale footprints of our culprit, a very large moose. We had been told this could happen, but had never seen it on our farm.

Moose are the bulldozers of the animal world, nerds of the North, morons

(David Aiken Photo)

of maple country. They can wreak havoc on a tubing system. The most maddening thing—moose are not even scared of us…THE AUDACITY!

By striking contrast, another part of the sugarbush had no tubing damage in it at all. We scurried from tree to tree and did our cleaning job in record time. This was the woods where the deer lived. They nested among the big maples down there, leaving nightly impressions in the leaf mold. I'd watched them navigate those woods, carefully nudging under the tubing lines or bounding over them. On one occasion, I even witnessed a buck angle his huge antlers this way and that way in deference to a short tubing span between two close trees.

Deer are graceful and beautiful. Most importantly, they hold great respect for the maple sugarmaker and his sugarbush appliances. Three cheers for the whitetails!

Mr. Moose reminded me of a story my father told about trucking Christmas trees to Florida. His big farm truck was loaded to the hilt when he headed out. The load was high and top-heavy and he recalled hearing a mysterious 'snap' somewhere deep in Georgia. The mystery was solved when he stopped a few miles later to check his load. There, to his horror, was a sizable portion of the town of Claxton's Christmas lights colorfully adorning his load of trees! Now I'm not comparing my father, who was a wonderfully intelligent man, to the Morse Farm moose; but if anyone spots a dumb moose somewhere in downtown White River Junction, the green maple tubing it's wearing, is mine! ❧

'48 Ford farm truck loaded high with Florida-bound Christmas trees. Harry Morse, Sr. stands on top.

Walking for the Ladies

I love the woods this time of year. There's a point between sugarin' and bug season, before the ferns start up, when the woods look groomed and the walking's easy. The post-fern woods look grizzled and walking's more like wallowing. Wildflowers come before the ferns.

Wildflowers are like gnomes of the flora world. They hide behind trees and watch for snow's final gasp before they creep out in the night. There's an order to their creeping; Spring Beauties come first, then Hepaticas, Bloodroot, Violets and Dutchman's breeches. Somewhere in that protocol lies the Red Trillium, my favorite. I love the name, "Red Trillium." It rings to my ears pretty and feminine, like the Katharine Hepburn of the flower world. It stands tall and elegant, save one major, troublesome blemish—someone back in history nicknamed it the "Stinkin' Benjamin!" Yesterday, I actually dropped to my knees at one of these beauties and gave a whiff. Neutral—my puzzlement goes on.

The Morses know their wildflowers. It started in the elementary school of Maple Corner with teachers like Mildred Bullock and Dot Morse. Those two taught the lion's share of three 'R's, but they also added a 'W' for "wildflower." No student of theirs, girl, boy, quick or slow, escaped the eighth grade without a complete knowledge of the local wildflowers. My 'W' is limited because I'm the youngest in my family and got denied, by the times, out of a full eight school years with one of those magnificent ladies.

One day I walked into my older brother Elliott's repair shop, stumped over the nomenclature of a flower. "You there, Elliott," I shouted, sensing presence under an ailing Volkswagen. He crept out, feet first, and wiped his hands with a greasy rag. I shoved my mystery bouquet in his face. By rote he spewed "Squirrelcorn, *Dicentra canadensis*—grows a little yellow bulb like a kernel of corn."

I thanked him, and then asked, narrowing my eyes like a private detective, "How'd the Red Trillium get that bad rap?"

"I guess you mean 'Stinkin' Benjamin,'" he chuckled. "I don't know—must've been some old Yankee a long time ago havin' a bad day!" I left, a little smarter about Squirrelcorn, but still puzzling over the Red Trillium.

My father's favorite wildflower was the Showy Lady Slipper. There's a Showy Lady Slipper swamp somewhere here in Central Vermont (I ain't goin'ta tell you where). My father went to the Lady Slipper swamp every year. Lady Slippers come out late, after the ferns and the bugs. The Showy is extremely rare and on

Mildred Bullock poses with her students at Maple Corner School, circa 1948.

all those trips, my father duly honored them, but for one minor transgression. He'd always pick a couple for my mother who refused to go because of the bugs.

The last time Harry went to the Lady Slipper swamp was the year before he passed away. He'd suffered the ravages of several strokes and needed help with everything. My brother Tick, determined that Father not miss the Lady Slippers, built a special chair with four handles. One evening in late May, we helped him into a four-wheel drive pickup and headed for the swamp. My sister, Susie, wielded her camcorder, a matter for which we are eternally grateful. We drove close to the swamp and four of us carried Father the rest of the way, sultan style.

Harry Morse sits amid his beloved Showy Lady Slippers.

Father, miss not the Lady Slippers
And so to the swamp we must go
The Showy is rare
With bugs and mud, do we dare?
Yes! We'll pick two for my lady, don't you know.

Recently we watched Susie's footage. It showed a tired looking Harry, shrunken by age and ailments. He sat in the cab of a Chevrolet pickup and grimaced as we lifted him into the sultan chair. We headed toward the swamp, willing the bugs away. When we reached the Showys, they were in perfect bloom. Father beamed

Men working the granite quarry in Adamant, Vermont, circa 1900.

for the first time in a very long time. We slogged ahead, our boots making deep, sucking sounds. We stopped at a place where the Showys were at their best and lowered him down. He reached out and picked just two. He turned toward Susie's camera and recited a rhyme that made us all laugh. It was a happy trip back to the truck. Harry had seen his beloved Showys one more time and in his positive way, probably never considered it might be his last. He'd just taken one more trip to the Lady Slipper swamp to pick a couple flowers for his favorite lady. 🍁

Rock Solid Friends

A few weeks ago I said goodbye to an old friend and partner up here in the Northeast. Although his face was craggy and graying and he was not the most handsome guy in the world, he did his job well and stood tall right to the end. He and I had been in the same business for a long time. You see, folks traveling this area would stop at his place before they came to mine, or vice versa. They remarked on how well he was doing or how much they looked forward to seeing him. Many times they missed him because he was away that day, but they always bought a keepsake of some kind with his picture on it.

He was among New England's most aged citizens. I am now fifty-five, and he was more than twice my age (Yes, it's true!). He was truly a universal character. His picture adorned everything from road signs to coins to license plates. It never went to his head. He was just glad to stay put and do his job. Few seasoned travelers in New England could forget the Old Man of the Mountain, that world famous granite profile over in Franconia Notch, New Hampshire.

Occasionally, he went away because of the thick, pea soup clouds that obscured him way up there above the Notch. On the night of May 2, 2003, the clouds had taken him away one more time. When dawn brought clear skies the next day, however, the Old Man was still gone. Millions of years of artistic perfection had come unglued and his lofty features tumbled to the mountain base sometime in the night. He had no real age. He was "of the times," but his clock stopped on our generation's watch, May 3, 2003.

I love nature's sculptures, especially ones made from rock. I make sculptures out of wood, but wood is too temporary. Rock lasts for, umm, I better not say forever, had I? Let's just say rock can last a long time. I especially admire any sculptor who would take on the tough medium of rock. Rock sculptors, God included, need all the artistic talent of any sculptor, but also bull strength and persistence. Wow!

I will miss the Old Man, but he is no different than droopy stone walls or moss covered cemetery stones. It was just art that served its time well

and then Nature had another plan. It seems Vermont and New Hampshire will be flat like Kansas some day if the mountains keep falling into the valleys. That's okay—somehow I feel assured when Nature does the drivin'. ❧

Jungle Life in Vermont

Two nights ago sleep was a problem. I don't remember the first dream, but in the second, a guy from New York had just bought a tractor from me. It fell off his trailer and smashed all over my mother's yard (nobody was hurt, thank God). Then I woke up. I stumbled across the dark house, one more trip to the refrigerator. Beyond my kitchen window, the night was still and moonlit, but suddenly all hell broke loose—a piercing, ghoulish racket sounded from the top of a small hemlock tree. The tree shook like we were having an earthquake, instantly jarring my sleepy memory into first gear. I had heard that commotion once before and knew it was raccoons in the trees.

Raccoons are 'two-faced' rascals. On the ground, they're quiet except for some occasional light chatter. They scour in the nighttime, programmed for fresh corn, but reasonably content with miscellaneous filth. That, and a little peace and quiet is all they really want. When something interrupts their routine, however, watch out! They'll hustle up the nearest tree and transform into screaming, screeching dervishes. They cry like monster babies and sing like Rod Stewart on steroids. I stood there, thankful for the barrier of glass protecting me from open warfare, grumbling about how my night was going. I reached for the switch and turned on the yard light. The tenor of the raccoons instantly changed, and they started their descent down the tree. I was surprised that they came down head first, unlike a bear. Four of them congregated on our walkway. When I rapped on the window, they quietly slinked into the night.

I puzzled over why they were up there in the first place, refusing to believe it was for the purpose of love; even a raccoon can't be that foolish! I considered a few workable possibilities before finally going back to bed, unwilling to analyze the life cycle and habits of *Procyon americanus* a second longer. Before I slept, however, I thought of the last creature that descended that same hemlock.

I had decided to clean my chimney on a late fall day. I donned my oldest, most tattered clothes, gathered my paraphernalia, and crept up to the roofline with my bucket loader. Farmers use their bucket loaders for everything. That day, it would be my ladder. I climbed to the pinnacle and began plunging the brush toward the chimney's bowels. Storm clouds of soot rose up, masking my eyes like a raccoon. Close by, I heard a faint eep…eep…eep…eepeepeep. I looked down and saw the bucket loader heading, driverless, toward the valley below. Damn—I hadn't set the emergency brake! I watched it nestle against some fir trees and stop.

I finished cleaning the chimney, worrying all the time about getting off that cussed roof. Nobody came to rescue me, and after two hours, I started thinking of alternatives.

(David Aiken Photo)

Finally, I fixed on that small hemlock tree which grew five feet from the roofline. "Could I possibly?" I thought, measuring the leaping distance in my mind and weighing the probability of broken bones against my humiliation. Skeptical, but desperate, I took a Tarzan lunge. My frantic clasp found the slender treetop. In perfect Robert Frost style, it flexed under my weight into a graceful arch. My descent to the ground was smooth and feet first, unlike a raccoon.

That hemlock's a handy little tree. Two times so far it's helped desperate creatures back to the sanity of terra firma. For that, I'm thankful. I'm also thankful for a great sound sleep last night, away from crashed machines and crazed animals. ❧

A Portrait in Safety

I didn't sleep well last night. Don't get me wrong—in Vermont, even a poor night for sleeping can be a pretty good night. At one point, I got up and went to our sliding glass door. I gazed out over the Winooski Valley and the town of Berlin's lights beyond. Berlin's colorful lights are created by multi-businesses, a hospital, an airport, and busy roads that lead to the rest of the world. I love that view from the safe distance of my home. Sometimes I fantasize about getting on a plane or taking one of those roads to exciting places. Last night I stayed and gazed longer than usual. There was a particular sparkle to the lights, a vibrancy that kept me glued to the scene. A million lightning bugs danced below and around those lights of civilization and from above, thousands of sparkling stars completed the frame. It was a perfect 3-D portrait called "Nature and Man in Harmony." Sometimes we forget that man and nature can, indeed, make beauty together. When I finally returned to my bed, sleep came easily. My final thoughts were of beauty and harmony in a safe place—and stories of man, nature, safety, and the middle of the night.

A few years ago, I was out on a frosty June night, irrigating my strawberries. One way to protect strawberry blossoms from frost is to irrigate them. I belonged to the East Montpelier Fire Department at the time, and my fire department garb seemed appropriate for the job. It was around 2:00 A.M. and I was dealing with a plugged sprinkler-head. When the sprinkler cleared I turned away to avoid a direct face wash. Up toward the highway, the headlights of a car were trained in my direction. As the blurry form of a person approached, I thought about the safety and warmth of my bed back home. I would have felt foolish were it not that my efforts were strictly in the line of duty. The form trudged nearer and nearer. When it got within rock-throwing range, I realized it was a person in uniform, a Vermont State Trooper. He cautiously approached, skeptical of my strange presence. My eyes went from his wide brimmed hat down past his official torso and finally settled on some mighty soggy pant bottoms.

"Sir," he said, policeman style, "I was passing by and saw your fluorescent EMFD down here in the middle of nowhere. I need to know what you're doing."

I wiped water from my eyes and burst out laughing. "Just doin' my duty, officer, much like you are!" I explained the science of freezing water as best I could. He quickly understood why I was dressed like a fireman and that I was just an innocent farmer. We both had a good laugh, and I thanked him as he turned to leave.

"You sure went above and beyond the call of duty this time, officer."

"Not at all," he said, "those strawberries will taste great in July."

Another time, my brother Elliott, our town's Cemetery Commissioner, was digging a grave in the middle of the night. He had tried to hire a backhoe, but found they were all employed at local construction sites. This left no choice, but to do it the old fashioned way and his deadline (excuse the pun) brought him to the task in the night. He was down in the grave with his head just level with the ground. All of a sudden two police cars came screaming up the road and pulled into the cemetery's parallel drives. One came in the upper one and blocked Elliott's truck from the east. The other blocked it from the other side. A lady officer approached first. She looked down and shined her flashlight right in his face.

Elliott leaned his shovel against the square wall of earth and said, "Ma'am, if you want me to come out with my hands up, you're goin' ta have ta give me a hand."

He was thankful for the visit because he had literally dug himself into a hole with no way out. He explained that the grave was to be occupied at 2:00 the following afternoon and that time was running out. When the two officers understood Elliott's innocence, they settled in for a good laugh, wished him a good night, and resumed their nocturnal patrol.

Yes, there's safety in 'them thar hills' up here in Vermont. There's also beauty and folks willing to do their jobs all hours of the day and night. Compared with much of the world, civilization is minimal here. There's lots of room for nature and man alike; we get along just fine. I hope to sleep better tonight but if I don't, I'll look to the stars and the lightning bugs and the airport lights, and dream of far away places. Sweet Dreams. 🍁

Two Vermont Characters

The other day I was out fixing fence. At long last our pastures were firming up after the spring thaw (a.k.a. Mud Season) and our animals were eyeing the green grass from their winter environs. They were anxious to get out there. It was one of those spring days that hinted of summer at its best. I had been hurrying, well aware of a million other things to do, when my back urged me to stretch and relax for a minute. I stood straight, put my nose to the air and allowed the Vermont goodness to filter into every pore. My mind shifted gears and a reverie, as pleasant as the day, took me away for a few minutes. When I returned, a yellow sea of dandelions pulled my eyes towards the horizon. It was a rude sounding cough, however, that reclaimed my focus. There, standing but thirty feet to my left, was a huge, dark moose. I have no idea how long he'd been there, but the fellow stood with a distinct lack of fear, in fact, seeming indifference. After our initial introduction, he reached down and tugged a clump of grass, roots and all, from the earth. He munched hungrily, keeping his eyes on mine.

When I was young, there were no moose in Central Vermont. They were creatures from the wilds of Maine that we read about in books. They appeared in comics, personified and dumb. They supplied antlers for random curiosity shops, but they were not here in the flesh until I reached my early twenties. Even though we have lots of them around now, folks still slow down when they see one. Moose have the reputation of being one of the stupidest animals alive. Some folks say they have a parasite that makes them crazy and they mate with cows! They certainly are unique beasts, bigger than anything else on four legs and outwardly tame. The moose is the only wild creature I know who stands firm in the presence of humans. I usually agree with the stupidity factor, but on this day, I saw a glimpse of intelligence in those dark eyes. As we stood and silently communicated, I sensed moose vibes and imagined a conversation that would have gone something like this:

(David Aiken Photo)

Moose: "My dear sir, you must watch out where you go. I'm bigger than you and might just knock you over."

Morse: "Wait just a minute, pal, you see I own this property!"

Moose, laughing: "Don't be ridiculous. Nobody owns this land and if they did, it would be someone big like me."

Morse: "Ya, sure. Tell that to the East Montpelier tax collector on November 14th. By the way, how long have your folks been here in Vermont?"

Moose: "We came over from Maine the last generation, but I was born here."

Morse: "Got'cha there—my Vermont roots go back seven generations."

Moose, hurrying to next subject: "Another thing that bothers me about you people. You zoom around in your four-wheeled projectiles and are a danger to society. Why don't you just lope like we do?"

Morse, under his breath: "With gas spiraling to over $3.00 a gallon, we'll all be loping soon enough."

Moose: "Well, I gotta move along. I live way over in Cabot where there's a nice lookin' Holstein I've had my eye on."

The last I saw of Mr. Moose, he was loping east toward Cabot. My eyes followed his bulk until a dark green bank of balsams parted, and then he was gone. He left me with a greater appreciation of his species and supplied me with one more pleasant contribution to the already great day. I shook my head, smiled, and went back to fencing. I had car payments to make and taxes to pay. 🍁

Louise wishes to remain incognito, but Burr's grandma, Mildred Morse, lived to be 97 thanks to a strong work ethic and a dash of maple syrup.

Something in the Water

We had a workday for our ski center last Saturday. I had sent out an invitation via e-mail to a group of skiers asking for their help. One of the volunteers who came was my good friend, David. He and I went to Montpelier High School together way back in the Dark Ages and it's always good to talk over old times with him. He arrived bright and early, and after we exchanged pleasantries he said, tongue-in-cheek, that his mother was upset with me. Dave's eighty-seven-year-old mother, Louise, had been to my place the day before and we'd had a good talk. It seems she was upset because I had not invited her to the workday. Wow! There is something in the water up here in Vermont—sap water. The rite of transition from winter's doldrums to spring's rebirth is a powerful thing for Vermonters. Maple syrup symbolizes things like rebirth, purity and goodness. Louise has participated in eighty-seven spring times and I know she loves her maple syrup. Of course, there's no guarantees of living to eighty-seven, but a good healthy work ethic and a dash of maple syrup won't hurt at all. Bless your heart, Louise! The next time I have a workday, you'll be invited for sure. 🍁

LEFT
Rope tow at Morse Farm in East Montpelier, 1960.

FOLLOWING PAGE
Precursor to the Morse Farm Cross-Country Ski Touring Center of today, Morse Farm had downhill skiing using a ropetow.

Shades of Gray and Hayfield Artillery

This morning as I fueled up my tractor, I looked over at the gray, metal roof we recently put on our barn. Except for three year's worth of ugly, off-white bird spatter on the black cupolas, the new roof matched well with the gray barn. Those cupolas glared at me and I wished we had painted them gray, like the roof. My mind strayed, logically, to the day I proudly showed my friend Ed, my brother's 1948 Ford tractor, which also sported a fresh coat of gray paint. Ed is a collector of those little gray Fords, that quintessential American farm tractor. As Ed admired the tractor he offered bits of Ford tractor trivia, including the reason old Henry Ford painted them gray. Gray is the only color that doesn't show bird droppings. I glanced back at the cupolas as I drove away from the fuel tank, bothered, but now thinking of Ford tractors.

I used to trade work with my friend Gerald Pease. He helped me with sugarin' in the spring and I helped him with haying in the summer. Gerald had one of those little gray Ford tractors. His was named "Speedy." Speedy was getting on in age when I served on the Pease Farm. She was Gerald's second tractor, surrendering the heavier duties of mowing and baling to Gerald's bigger, more stable John Deere. Speedy's personality quirks included a lack of brakes and faster than normal gearing, two qualities slightly unbecoming to Gerald's steep and rocky terrain. I recalled two noteworthy episodes with Speedy, one which occurred before my

(Marne Rizika Ilustration)

time and another which found Speedy and me embarrassed accomplices.

One day before I started going over there, Speedy was pulling a load of hay into Gerald's barn. Gerald's barn was typical of Vermont barns with a downstairs stable and an upstairs haymow, accessible by an upward sloping ramp called a "highdrive." Because of Speedy's high gearing and low power, it was necessary to approach the highdrive with a considerable head of steam. She made it up the highdrive, bumped over the threshold, and onto the haymow floor. That day, by a bad stroke of luck or possibly the

Gathering hay, pre-Speedy.

absence of brakes, Speedy continued past the haymow and right through the other side of the barn. When she stopped, she dangled vertically against the barn wall, anchored to the hay wagon which had stopped inside. Gerald said the driver was clinging to the steering wheel and white as a sheet, but unharmed.

The other Speedy episode found me guilty of Yankee ingenuity and poor judgment at the same time. We were scrambling to get a field of hay dried and baled, ahead of a looming rainstorm. The hay was dry on the surface, but needed to be turned over. For this we employed a machine called a "tedder." Gerald was pulling his new tedder with the John Deere, and I had nothing to do until the hay was dry enough for me to begin raking it with Speedy. As I waited, my workaholic nature found me looking for ways to help. My eyes settled on an old horse drawn "kicker" that rested in retirement by the stonewall along the field's edge. A kicker, the tedder of its day, consisted of a series of hayforks rigged on a crankshaft.

Burr with sister, Susie, up to "no-good" in the hayfield.

The hayforks kicked out in an alternating fashion as the crankshaft revolved, moved by steel wheels which conveyed the entire contraption and turned as the horses pulled it along. It was a great tool for its time, but was designed for horses, not tractors.

"Could I convert the kicker to a tractor hitch," I thought, already reaching for the tools. Half an hour later, Speedy and I arrived in Gerald's hayfield pulling the old kicker which was set in the neutral position. Proud as anything, I drove to a point untedded, stopped and levered the kicker into gear. Gerald rounded a corner just in time to dodge kicker parts flinging at him "dart fashion" from every direction. When I finally stopped and looked behind me, that kicker was reduced to an unrecognizable pile of scrap and the rest of my day was spent separating metal fragments from the hay, in the rain. Speedy was just too speedy for that old kicker that worked so well in slower times. 🍁

The Power of Dandelions

Dandelions! They blanket our Vermont countryside this time of year. You'd think I'd be happy to accept their springtime yellow as a pleasant alternative for winter's white, but somehow I can't always warm up to them. Dandelions are the schizophrenics of the flora world. Singularly they're pretty; exponentially, they're ugly as sin. There's nothing cuter than a grinning toddler stumbling up to you, offering a crumbled bouquet of dandelions. That always seems to happen on a beautiful sunny day and you're always glad to be alive. I defy anyone, however, to identify a single dandelion merit by the meadow-full. There's something about their collective hue that just doesn't cut the mustard, and then it gets worse. Instead of going away, they painfully wilt into those annoying, fluffy domes. And then, when they do go away, well— they don't. This morning I mowed the lawn. My trusty John Deere does a pretty good job with anything green in spite of its dull blades, but late season dandelions are impossible to cut. Now demoted to stiff pale spears, they stand like little warriors, thumbing their noses at the very idea of manicure. This morning I did battle with the last of those devils, or did I?

With dandelions, we're not just talking aesthetics. Oh no, they're multi-dimensional creations. It seems they contribute to every area of our lives, including culinary, social, medicinal, romantic, and psychological. As you now know, they bring out a bit of the obsessive-compulsive in me (those cussed little spears!).

A study in age and pullin' out dandelions. Little Peter Shattuck and Ernest Gould.

My father told about an old doctor who said there was more medicinal value in one serving of dandelion greens than in his entire doctor's bag.

Yes, you cut those rascals right at the root line when they're young and succulent, and they're edible to about 1% of the human population—I'm in that group. And there are others who enjoy them in a liquid form.

Harry I. Morse in various stages of youth, always close to where the dandelions grow.

One time my father employed his toddling grandchildren to scurry about our property picking dandelion blossoms. He wanted to make dandelion wine and, being a caring Grandpa, organized it as a family affair. I'll always remember those bobbing, blond heads against a vast sea of yellow, and most especially, the copious amounts brought to Father's penny-a-blossom checkpoint. He paid them off, sent them home, and then made a massive batch of wine. Sometime later that summer our friends, Ben and Jeanne, came for a visit from down-country. Father used the occasion to debut his wine at an August corn roast. It was a cool and moonlit night, perfect in every respect. The wine met with delirious reviews. In fact, it was so good that Jeanne got a little giggly. When the party ended, Ben and Jeanne left, very pleased with Vermont hospitality. The next time we saw them was the following year around dandelion time. They came into our store carrying newborn baby Greg. Jeanne went right up to my father, wagged her finger in his face: "Harry Morse, you're responsible for this. Greg was conceived the night of the corn roast and it was your wine that did it!"

Since that time ten trillion dandelions have come and gone and Greg is a hulking twenty-six-year-old. The dandelions are finally giving way, for this season, to the buttercups and daisies. Buttercups and daisies are much prettier by the meadow-full, but as we all know, beauty is only skin-deep. They don't supply surprises and keep our adrenaline pumping like the lowly dandelion. 🍁

A Baleful Story

The other day I saw a modern farmer out baling hay. He drove his large tractor from the comfort of a climate-controlled cab. Behind the tractor a machine gobbled hay from double windrows and randomly deposited huge bales around the field, like super-sized shredded wheat. The sweet smell of fresh hay powered my nostalgia back to haying in the 1950s, when I was growing up on our small, side hill farm.

Besides milking cows, we had a farm machinery dealership on our place. The brand we sold was Allis-Chalmers. This company made the best darned tractors in the whole world, a quality highlighted by their bright pumpkin-orange color. Back in those days names of tractors were far less important than colors. In a field of Farm-All reds, John Deere greens, and Case yellows, orange always won the pulling contests, treads down. Unfortunately, there was a downside to the Allis image—they made terrible implements. To add insult to injury, Allis-Chalmers

On Mountain Goat, an "Elliott" built machine, Tick Morse, two friends, and Elliott Morse.

tractors had a unique hitch design that meant those folks hooked on the world's best tractors had to use the world's worst implements! The most notorious Allis-Chalmers implement of all was their roto-baler.

The roto-baler was both ahead of its time and behind the eight ball—a hayfield loser in a square bale world. It attempted to produce a rolled bale from dried hay, a concept virtually doomed by the limited technology of those times, the tangling nature of hay, and a thing called Murphy's Law. It was a weird looking contraption that resembled, from most angles, more a mobile outhouse than a piece of farm machinery. We pulled ours with an Allis WD tractor with Armstrong steering and a steel seat that matched the contours of a farmer's butt. The seat extended out behind the rear wheels, affording a quick and frequently used escape route for the poor soul who drove. The roto-baler was hitched to the tractor by a long pole accompanied by a vicious power–take-off shaft. Cocked to one side, a wide conveyor directed hay to a swirling mass of rollers, belts, and gears. For some reason, the thing had to stop and strain every time it discharged, with results ranging from a stringy mass, to a tiny plug, to nothing at all. Think of a giant, roaring creature with stomach problems.

My brother Elliott got the best of those roto-balers at an early age. He is naturally mechanical and learned quickly from our Uncle Bernard who could twist, bend, fabricate, or curse into action any machine part under the sun. Elliott settled into the job of repairing roto-balers like a socket to a lugnut. At sixteen, he traveled all over Washington County performing his mechanical magic and baling whole fields for distraught farmers. One farmer called threatening to "jump in the cussed thing if that kid didn't get there PDQ!" My brother went on to make a career of repairing Volkswagen Beetles, hooked for a lifetime it seems, on machines weird in appearance and design.

Elliott Morse on an Allis-Chalmers G.

To use a well-seasoned cliché, times have changed. Allis-Chalmers orange now sit rusting in junkyards, or spruced up for collectors. Volkswagen Beetles (the real ones, not the modern day wannabes) rolled into the history books about the time Elliott Morse packed up his tools for good. Farmers no longer dismount tractors from the rear, but through side doors and down three steps. They get off to make cell calls or stretch—field work for modern farmers is more boredom than breakdown. That farmer I saw the other day was baling up a storm. Those bales he made were big and, by God, they were ROUND! Yes, technology has finally untangled the mysteries of haying equipment. Round is in. Square is out. How's that for full circle? 🍁

A Trip to Hardwick

The road to Hardwick.

Last week I traveled up to Hardwick to attend the funeral of a good friend, Bob Brown. My old truck clattered up County Road, through Maple Corner, and on to Woodbury Gulf, my favorite road in the whole world. As I passed the height of land where Calais becomes Woodbury and looked to the edge of the swamp, I could see the fiddleheads, (early growth of the Ostrich Fern), were ready. I made a mental note to stop on my way back through and pick a mess for supper. I pressed on toward Hardwick.

Nearing the funeral home, I discovered that Bob's popularity was causing a parking problem. I finally found a place out back of the Town Garage and as I left the truck, I glanced in the back at two hemlock planks, a few bottles I'd picked up on the roadside, and my iron bar. I walked across the tracks and joined the overflow crowd on the back porch of the funeral home. There, twenty of us stood, somber, hearing only bits and pieces of the service inside. Alone with my thoughts, I concluded that Bob would probably find this all quite foolish, possibly saying, "God, don't drive all the way to Hardwick for just a funeral; do something else while you're theyah."

Soon folks started coming out and I returned to my truck. There on the driver's seat was a note that read: "borried your iron bar to bush my peas. won't have it long. Willis T Shatney." I looked around and in the distance saw a person working in the freshly plowed earth. I walked toward the person, noticing as I neared that it was an old man, slightly stooped, and punching holes in the earth with my bar. As I reached him, his rhythm halted, and he presented me with the biggest hand I'd ever shaken, a hand made only by spending a lifetime milking cows. It seemed he had sold his farm a year ago and moved to the village. His bar had sold in the auction, and he'd walked by my truck while I was at the funeral

Maple Corner, circa 1948. Road to Hardwick.

and saw my bar in the back. He just seemed to know, probably by the personality of the truck, that I wouldn't mind if he borrowed it. He was right.

I stayed and helped him finish his pea bushing. He punched holes and I shoved a brush into each one for the pea vines to climb on. Wordlessly, we finished the last row and he handed the bar to me. "Much obliged, young man," he said, as we parted company. I felt good on my way back down the Gulf that day. I stopped to pick a mess of fiddleheads for supper and knew that Bob would approve. 🍁

Air Enhancement in Vermont

Sidney Bennett Morse, 1894–1973.

Sidney Morse's "empire" in East Montpelier, Vermont, circa 1955.

We finished boiling sap a while back for this season, cleaned up the evaporator, and filed that wonderful aroma under "C" for "Can't wait." On one of the last days, a lady from up the road came in to get one last whiff. I recognized her from past visits and knew of her special love for sugarin'—some Vermonters have maple in their DNA, you know. She breathed in extra deeply, head tilted heavenward. As she exhaled, she looked at me squarely and said: "I have to open all my car windows when I go by this place, you know. I can't pass without letting that wonderful smell in." That particular morning my mind was sharp as a well-honed tapping bit. I saw where this could go. "Of course," I said, "we have the opposite of air pollution here. In Vermont we have air enhancement concerns." I went on to say that the legislature had actually drawn up a commission to create a Vermont Air Enhancement Index. On a scale of 1 to 10, sugarin' would be a 10, lilac blossoms, 9.9, first cutting of alfalfa, 9.5, January on a bad day, 9.4," she interrupted me, "Burr, are you sure this isn't a bull enhancement index?" I smiled. "Ma'am, you may have something there."

Each spring at the end of sugarin', my grandfather and I picked a good rainy day to clean out the bullpen (not to be confused with anything to do with baseball). Back then, before the days of technicians with accessories, farmers always kept a service bull. Our bull's name was Sparky. Sparky resided in a ten by twelve foot pen out in the old barn. With a guarantee of plenty of work and two squares a day, he stayed quite happy. Like most bulls, however, he had little use for people. Because of this, daily maintenance of his pen was entirely unworkable. We gave him wide berth and only mucked him out when his backbone neared the ceiling. Cleaning the bullpen was a job I savored because I got to do it with Grandpa Morse. Grandpa was a small man with big stories and huge common sense. On

cleaning day we approached Sparky with a long hooked bull staff. Quick as a matador, Grandpa thrusted out the staff and hooked it into Sparky's nose ring. This done, Sparky was instantly transformed from a snorting man-hater to a 2,000 pound pussycat. I remember swelling with pride when Grandpa handed him over to me for a quiet stroll to temporary quarters.

I didn't realize it at the time, but that experience added volumes to my nostalgia

Sidney Morse feeding chickens.

LEFT
Training two young oxen.

library. My time spent with Grandpa was filled with invaluable lessons, like feeling pride in doing a good job. I even learned a few things from old Sparky. Beyond those teachings lies something much more down to earth; something only a farmer may truly understand. You see, I love the texture of rotting bull manure. I love the feeling of stabbing a sharp dung fork into its rich darkness and pitching it into a waiting spreader. I love its promise of green grass. There, I said it! Bull manure carries to my senses a pleasant "sweetness," almost like a delivery of fresh hay.

I'm so grateful for the memories from old Sparky, wherever he is and—oh, as for his contribution to the air enhancement index—I'd give him at least a 9. 🍁

Munger's Magic

It was Summer 1956, and a group of kids strolled along a country road in Putney, Vermont. The July heat draped around them like a warm wet towel. They moved along slower than usual taking little comfort from the parched maples which hung overhead. Suddenly there was a rumbling close enough and powerful enough to interrupt the lazy sounds of the cicadas. The kids knew instinctively what it was and spilled toward the road's edge. They gathered behind huge maple trunks and hedge-line boulders, and plugged their noses and eyes against the choking gravel dust. The beast thundered by in a whirlwind. When the air finally settled they abandoned their positions, one at a time, and regrouped

Beatrice Howard Aiken and Malcolm Jones, Jr., "Mac" in story.

where they started. They looked toward the receding rumble and resumed their lazy frolic. "Whew. That was a close one," one of them said to a chorus of agreement. The beast that flashed by was a tattered '52 Plymouth. Behind the wheel was Beatrice Howard Aiken, my grandmother. I was one of those kids who was there that day.

We called her Munger because my mother, who'll be ninety-one on her next birthday, couldn't say "mother"—strange how these things get started. Munger was always helping folks, and she ran that '52 Plymouth ragged. She removed all but the driver's seat to facilitate hauling everything from cupboards to bushels of apples to families of snapping turtles. She provided sap buckets for the occasional passenger to sit on and I remembered the first time I rode on her sap bucket seats. We headed for a neighbor's place to battle with 10,000 potato bugs and my sister, Susie, and I were to be front line soldiers. We each chose a sap bucket and readied ourselves for the ride. Munger got behind the wheel, started up the Plymouth and "floored" the poor thing unmercifully. Being a farm boy and knowing something about engines, I envisioned the aging crankshaft heading right into orbit. When the roar finally subsided, she turned to us and said with a smile, more like a cartoon character than a grandmother, "You gotta blow the soot outa these darn things once in a while." To Susie and me, already quite giggly over the sap bucket seats, that was hilarious!

Bea Aiken lived like she drove—fast paced and with purpose. Always a champion of the underdog, she smelled out folks in need almost before they were aware of it themselves. Her generosity knew no bounds. She was forever dropping off furniture and canned goods for families in need and usually did it incognito. One time she took in two brothers, fifteen and seventeen, who had fled Hungary. She taught them English and raised them as her sons until both went off, American citizens to American colleges. Another time she and her young daughter, Barbara, cleaned the gutters and milked the cows for a farm family in need. Young Barbara complained that she never had milked a cow before.

"Why Tot," (Munger gave everyone names that made no sense but stuck for a lifetime) she said, "just grab two of those hangin' things and pull until they stop leakin'!"

She loved the church, but was forever tweaking it for perfection. Heck, she even tweaked the minister on occasion. She tried hard to hide her goodness "under a bushel," but it never worked. Bushels in her world usually overflowed with the fruits of her own labors and had no room to hide anything. She was the wife of U.S. Senator, George Aiken, who spent much of his time in Washington away from bushels and tattered Plymouths. He was traditionally famous and the subject of a recent book, *The Essential Aiken*.

My grandmother never had a book written about her but, by God, she should have. She was untraditionally famous. If it weren't for her, the Senator never could have gone to Washington and done all those great things for mankind. She stayed home and "minded the farm," which included their thriving nursery business, an apple orchard, and all the Vermont stuff that couldn't be managed from a distance. She supported him on every front, even when it meant going to Washington for bill signings and White House events. She knew the way there—she also knew the way home. My Aunt, Tot, recently said, (modern day women must be sitting down for this). "Before he entered politics, he would go to the Aiken Nursery every day in a shirt and tie. He would get up, dress, and come into the kitchen where Ma would tie his tie and wash his glasses." SHE WASHED HIS GLASSES!

Aunt Tot also said Munger had a political side. At election time she'd provide transportation to the polls hoping, of course, her passengers were mostly Republicans. She never told anyone how to vote unless they asked. When they did, she was glad to honor their request, starting with 'A' for 'Aiken.' Tot said toward the end of the day she'd look at the checklist and go after those who hadn't voted yet.

One time Munger and my cousin Mac, were driving to our house in Montpelier. Mac, just a teenager, was behind the wheel. Every once in a while Munger would lean toward the speedometer and say, "Push it along. Push it along." That about sums up Beatrice Howard Aiken, my grandmother. She was a "push it along" kind of person and accomplished much in seventy–one short years. She's the only person I ever knew who could tell a teenager to drive faster, a minister to shape up, a U.S. Senator to straighten his tie, and be loved by all. She was a wonderful, Vermont person who worked out world problems right here at home. 🍁

Hang Gliding in the Pea Field

Here it was the middle of May and the ground was white with snow that morning! It had rained (or snowed) for three days and the temperature was lower than my tractor stuck in mud. We were trying to plant our six acres of sweet corn. We plowed and harrowed the ground weeks ago when the weather hinted of summer. Then a fleet of huge manure trucks showed up from a local dairy farm and "sweetened" the acreage, but Murphy's Law set in with a vengeance. We sat, one week later, eyeing the cornfield with the anticipation of planting, some day, when the ground dried enough to get near it with the corn planter.

This wait reminded me of my earlier days on the Morse Farm when we were planting a wide variety of vegetable crops. My father, rest his soul, was an avid market gardener who was ultra-creative in dealing with the trials of crop farming this rocky, cantankerous farm. Harry Morse never let something as untamable as the weather or the lay of the land get him down. In his latter years, he registered ten on the Richter Scale of positive thinking, probably because successful vegetable farming meant that he would never have to milk another cow as long as he lived.

One memory that stands out in my mind was of my father's pea pickin' system. Peas were always the first crop we planted because they will tolerate, in fact, thrive on, the cold weather of early summer. Many years the little, green fellers would poke up through an inch of snow and, barring an early harvest

Harry side-dressing sweet corn, another of Harry's inventions.

Harry handling silage the hard way.

by our neighbors, the woodchucks, would be ready for picking by mid June. Harry was always ready to pick peas. We planted the variety that produced prolifically, but low to the ground. My father, refusing to kneel or pick on his knees, wired a flat plywood bottom to an old milking stool so that the legs would not jab into the ground. He sat, picked, and scooted up and down the rows.

Pea pickin' went right on, rain or shine for Harry. For those rainy days he fabricated a contraption from light board strapping and plastic sheeting. It had a cross beam centered just above his head so he could alternately scoot, pick, and move the contraption ahead. We called it "Harry's pea pickin' hang glider." He never became airborne, but he sure enjoyed covering a lot of ground.

Harry had his own favorite story about a unique approach to vegetable farming. He told of old Kenneth Flowers up the road, who chose dynamite one year to dust his potato crop. "Kenneth," Harry reported, "placed a charge of dynamite in a grain sack, along with some potato dust. He then tied it to a fence post centered in the potato field and touched it off from a distance." "Well," Harry said, "He went a little too heavy on the dynamite; the potato crop ended up in the next county and Kenneth enjoyed his new pond for the rest of his years after the hole filled with water!"

Now you know Harry Morse got a little inventive with his stories like he did his pea picking. One thing for sure, though, he never did have to milk another cow. 🍁

You Gotta be a Little Nuts

Burr, away from facts and figures, doing what he loves.

The woods beckon. My inner voice, the louder one, says "Go." I load up the chainsaw, don my gear and head out, ignoring the weaker voice that says "cash flow, P&L charts, and bottom line." I have seven miles of cross-country ski trails to cut before snow flies. The mosquitoes don't care. I don't care. My buzz is bigger than theirs and they stay back. I love the woods. I am free!

My roots sink deep in this Vermont soil where trees are everywhere. I grew up with a chainsaw in my hand, like a third appendage. It gets me wood to heat my house, wood to boil my sap, wood to build my barn, and wood for my folk art. Yes, one of my little kinks is finding trees that look like something, refining them with my chainsaw, and ending up with a sculpture. So far I've got several different animals, some old curmudgeons, and my most famous one, Venus de Maple. Every once in a while I find a tree shaped like a letter of the alphabet and my goal is to spell a word before I die.

About twenty years ago I found an "N" over in the Crawford Lot. Then I found a "T" down in the south pasture and in 1998 an "S" jumped out of a big leverwood tree just before my saw made it two apostrophes; the only thing keeping me from spelling the word "nuts," was the letter "U." Then one day my life became complete because I found my "U!"

One of Burr's "literary" creations from the woods.

Now all that remains is to bolt those blessed letters to the side of my barn with a plaque that explains it all and ends something like this: 'And you gotta be a little nuts to spend fifty plus years spelling one four letter word!'

As I walk out of the woods, I stop at the babbling brook. And then it hits me. Taking a dollar from my billfold, I lean over and place it in the water. Watching it sail down stream, I begin to laugh hysterically, muttering, "cash flow." You gotta be a little nuts! 🍁

Tar Baby Vermont Style

Arrrrrrrrrgh! That's how my brother Elliott sounded one day last week. It all had to do with good old Frog Run—it'll grow hair on your chest and cure some of what ails you. They used to use it as flavoring for chewing tobacco and it's great for baked beans. It's not, however, recommended for your bubble bath. We have three table grades of maple syrup and one cooking grade; those are the ones you can buy. The one you can't buy is Grade C, Commercial, bud run, black strap—or to use the Vermonter's euphemism of choice—Frog Run.

Frog Run is the last syrup we make in our fleeting sugarin' season. The top four grades are made earlier, before the buds come out, when the weather is cool enough to preserve the sap. Good, well-preserved sap boils to a light colored, delicate flavored grade of syrup. Our four top grades are stable, once they are boiled to eleven pounds per gallon. They keep nicely in your refrigerator, ready to adorn any stack of pancakes on call, any time of year. Frog Run, our maverick grade, is quite unpredictable and sometimes downright ornery. It has a particular disdain for "consumer friendliness," the real reason you can't buy it. You see, Frog Run is made when our sugar season has turned sour, literally. When the day temperature rises above sixty degrees for a few days in a row, and the frogs wake up and start singing, sugarin' presents its last hurrah, the Frog Run.

Some folks refuse to make it—they simply quit sugarin'—but being old Scotch Yankees, we usually hang in to make a stock of Frog Run syrup. We keep the best of it to use in some of our blended products. The worst of it, we ship off to "one of those commercial syrup makers." There is nothing better than good Frog Run syrup, with its dark, robust flavor, to sweeten maple creemees and maple kettle corn. And there is nothing worse than bad Frog Run.

On that fateful day last week, Elliott was looking for some good dark syrup to flavor maple creemees. He had just cleaned the creemee machine. He was anxious to get to the woods and resume cutting his firewood. Unsuspecting the awesome power of a barrel of Frog Run that had "worked" for four months, he cracked the bung on the first barrel he approached. It was then that I heard his awful scream. When I got to him, Elliott looked like a character in the latest Sci-Fi movie. Fingers of ooze seeped down his forehead, over eyebrows and earlobes.

His trousers stuck to his skeleton and he walked like a zombie. He managed a feeble laugh through clenched lips and I joined in, of course. The last I saw him, he was laboring, one step at a time, down the road toward his house for some creative cleansing. I chuckled to myself, "Elliott, whatever you do, just don't go near that briar patch!" 🍁

Henry Ford Meets Bill Gates

The other day my friend and part-time employee, Claude, was up working on the new "Point of Purchase" (POP) computer system we were setting up at Morse Farm Maple Sugarworks. Earlier in the summer he had installed the "Mail Order Manager" (MOM) that took over for a program called the "Wizard," that wasn't so darn smart after all. Claude is a retired IBM'er, who walked away years ago with a gold watch and a world of knowledge. He had been applying his e-wisdom at the Morse Farm for several years now. As Claude explained how the new systems would eventually tie together, using words like "router, modem, and darn that Verizon." I politely stood by as a sluggish learner and writer of checks. You see, I accepted the idea that computers were necessary to carry Morse Farm into the future, but there was still this little feeling deep down in my seven generation Vermont roots that said, "Why?" Claude had just prompted the electronic cash drawer to open with a jingle when another noise led our attention to the front yard. My brother Tick was driving by in his Model T.

The "T" proved a perfect diversion from the brain work offered by our computers. We rushed out to find that beautiful black machine stopped by my mother's house. It made a striking contrast against the blue horizon. Claude gravitated to the "T" like a kid to a candy store and talk quickly ensued of magnetos, rag tops, and spoke wheels. Graciously accepting Tick's offer of a ride, we piled in and headed up Cummings Road, East Montpelier's ancient, dirt thoroughfare. The Model T was partial to the dirt road and our conversation was easy. Model T's speak more in a soft clatter than a roar. When I asked if I could drive, Tick explained the controls are different from modern vehicles. I couldn't just slip into the driver's seat. I thought to myself, "Humm—computers, Model T's—I can't drive either one!" Tick explained how "T's thrived on 'lugging' to painfully low RPMs on the hills, a distinct contrast to modern day engines." "If they made it to the top just ahead of stalling, that was perfect," he said.

Gerald Pease in Tick Morse's restored Model T.

We followed roads that led back to the Morse Farm from the north that day. As we chugged into our upper driveway I noticed, one more time, the blushing foliage. It exquisitely framed our view to the south of yonder hills and Montpelier's small airport. There was a plane in the sky headed for some distant place. We thanked Tick for the ride and took one final look at the magnificent machine as we headed back to our routers and modems. I knew that my computer learning would be different now after that day rife with entertainment and insight.

Computers are just tools to help us get from point A to point B, sort of a Model T for another time. When I went to bed that night, I thought of the book of Ecclesiastes: "There is A Season, Turn, Turn, Turn." Change is good. 🍁

Frost Heave Therapy

Wow, that hurt! I'd just tackled one of those 350-pound drums of maple syrup. I approached it like Attila the Hun, poised to muscle it to the upright position. There was just one problem—it was empty! I went head over heels and found myself splayed out like a bearskin rug on the sugarhouse floor. "I've done it now," I muttered, using some other words, too. I had twisted my knee, the same knee that troubled me since pre-sugar season. I had been walking like an old man, fearful that any wrong move would render me totally useless. I laid there, thoughts of leg braces and knee replacements filtering through the pain. After a few minutes, I picked myself up and timidly tried out my legs. Surprisingly, they worked. I stretched, amazed that the pain wasn't worse and resumed my sugarhouse cleaning. I forgot about the pain. Sometime later, I remembered the fall, but, strangely, my knee felt good.

My right knee troubled me for a long time. The snowshoe work of getting ready to sugar was particularly hard on it this year. In fact, I had finally asked

Chris, my friend who wanted to be a logger, but ended up an orthopedic surgeon, about an office visit. Then I had that therapeutic fall in the sugarhouse—yes, therapeutic. I must have twisted my knee just the right way because, except for the initial shock and some immediate pain, the fall had indeed made my knee better. I called Chris and said I would not need that office visit, much as my father Harry did not need a second one for his back.

Harry had a chronic bad back. I grew up seeing an array of back braces and wide belts strewn throughout the house. It seemed he had

Early back therapy.

a different appliance for changes in each workday and barometric pressure. By the frequent look of pain on his face, however, I was sure that none of them worked very well. One time he went to Burlington to a back specialist and was told he needed a major operation. The doctor said without the operation, he would soon be an invalid.

"That guy just doesn't understand," my father said." I can't afford the time, and I can't afford the money—guess I'll think it over."

It was the spring of the year. Sugarin' had just ended and our cows needed bedding. We used sawdust in those days for bedding and the nearest place to get

Farm truck hauled milk away from our farm, sawdust to our farm, and even fixed bad backs.

it was Berlin, New Hampshire, seventy-five miles northeast of our farm. My father, never one to let pain order him around, pulled himself up into the big farm truck the day after his diagnosis and headed out for Berlin. The truck, next of kin to a lumber wagon, bucked and bounced down County Road and eastward over a sea of frost heaves. I remembered him saying his back felt pretty good when he got there, in spite of his rough ride. He loaded up with sawdust and drove home over the same bumps, now magnified in a loaded truck. His back was so much better when he arrived home that he unloaded the whole thing, single-handedly, and headed back for another load.

"When I drove in the yard with the second load," my father said, "I felt spry as a youngster. By God, my back was cured by those bumps. I called that Burlington doctor and told him to forget about that operation and I never looked back."

My father passed away in 1999. He was eighty-two-years-old and in poor shape, but his back was not one of his problems. Forty years earlier, he had received some special therapy in the cab of a farm truck. No doubt about it—those New England frost heaves fixed Harry Morse's back just like my sugarhouse tumble fixed my knee. No, I'm not putting down modern medicine. I'm all for it, but sometimes when you have farmin' to do, the answer lies in something more natural. ❧

Give Pease a Chance

August 11 was my friend, Gerald Pease's birthday. It was also the day we buried him one year ago. Gerald was eighty-eight-years-old and had lived a wonderful life over on Culver Hill in Middlesex. It was quite appropriate that Gerald's birthin' and dyin' dates coincided like that—he loved getting together for whatever reason. His final gathering was in Shady Rill Baptist Church, also known as the little church that Gerald built. People packed in tighter than bales on a hay wagon and many dressed like Gerald would have, in white T-shirts and denim overalls. The service was light because stories of Gerald Pease brought laughter, not tears. We sang his favorite hymns, but reserved the most appropriate song for North Branch Cemetery when we lowered him in its stony soil: "Happy

Gerald Pease—farmer, jokester, friend to all.

birthday, dear Gerald." Gerald was, indeed, a dear man. He was also a "Deere" man. You see, he was born with poor eyesight and never drove a car. He traded in the reins of a horse at an early age for the steering wheel of a John Deere. Throughout Gerald's life he had multi-generations of John Deeres, all named and pampered. They not only worked for him and took him places, but they were his friends.

I first met Gerald when I was a teenager. It was sugar season and he came over to help. There were huge flakes of snow in the air. He got out of my father's car dressed in green woolen pants and laced up boots. Suspenders hitched somewhere in the middle of an ample belly and disappeared over two huge shoulders. On top of the shoulders sat a reddish face topped by a bright orange hat with funny earflaps. The hat's bill curved upward in a goofy fashion, away from thick, fogged up glasses. He reached a huge, callused paw in my direction and said, "How do?" I didn't know it at the time, but I had just met my best friend.

"Sap going to run today?" I asked. "Got two chances," he paused, "It either will or it won't." His high-pitched cackle shattered the ice in the driveway's puddles.

It didn't take long to divvy up our separate traits. He had a teenager with everything to learn. And I got a mentor and a crash course in respect. Gerald's somber side came early and was short lived—said he woke up depressed one morning when he was young. "I just made up my mind to start laughing at everything," he said, and, by God, he pulled it off.

Our long working relationship was blessed with trademark 'Geraldisms' like the "two chances" line. He milked them wherever he went, like his herd of cows which numbered twelve at its highest. Sometimes he'd call at 5:00 in the morning with the high-pitched greeting, "You're lookin' good…" Driven by respect, I always pretended I'd been up for a while, but most folks got downright mad. The night Betsy and I were married, he congratulated us with a handshake and prophesied of two chances. Luckily, after twenty-seven years, we're still opting for the former. Those years were, indeed, blessed through the friendship of this great man.

Ellen Pease— sister to Gerald, and wonderful friend.

He was never married except to his farm. He lived with his older sister, Ellen, and stayed put, except a few times when he got on a train and went away. One time he went clear to Russia. I asked him once how he pulled that off on a train. He answered with the most famous Geraldism of all, "Ha, Ha, Ha…How 'bout that!"

Betsy and I went over to see his sister, Ellen, back on Gerald's birthday. As we drove up the lane that led to his house, Gerald's fields looked well groomed and deep green. We parked by the ancient shed where his two John Deeres stood waiting for the next workday. The place looked great, almost like Gerald was still there. Ellen was glad to see us. She talked about the weather, all the hay that had come in from the fields and what a good job Sarah was doing. You see, Gerald sold the farm a few years ago to Sarah Seidman, lock, stock, and manure spreader. He knew she'd take good care of it. He was wise that way, and in most other ways that really matter. In fact, there was only one place his wisdom ever fell short. He always said when it came to heaven he had two chances, but he was wrong—there's only one place Gerald Pease went and he's up there right now saying, "HA, HA, HA…How 'bout that!" 🍁

The Demographics of Varmints

I've picked corn around here for forty years and saw a lot of changes along the way. For one thing, those full sacks sure weigh more than they used to. And varmints. We've got more varmints in our sweet corn than you could throw a stalk at; earwigs, earworms, ear borers, and the biggest pain in the ear of all, the ravenous raccoon!

There are more of them than there used to be and they have absolutely no scruples. At least a worm'll warn you it's comin' for a visit, but not these ring-tailed Rommels. They'll slink in under the radar to sample for maturity and flavor (they have human taste buds, you know). On the appointed night, they'll move in for complete cornfield annihilation, cob, stock and tassel.

I'd tried and failed at everything from salt licks to junkyard dogs until my father-in-law, Gil, came along. Gil Parker was a great man—friend of farmers, enemy of varmints, and crafty as all get out. Because of a chronic bad back, he worked in an office for the Agriculture Department, a frustrated farmer at heart.

One time Gil appeared just as I pushed a plate of cat food into the back of a box trap.

"See you're tryin' for skunks." he said. "Nope," I replied, frustrated. "Those ring-tailed devils are wipin' me out!"

He went on to explain that you had to target your audience when trapping animals. He said grapes were the perfect raccoon bait and told how he found out.

Gil Parker,
agriculture specialist
and varmint trapper.

"A friend and I were out one night years ago drinking beer. It was in the autumn and somehow we ended up at an abandoned house. In the moonlight we saw it was covered with grapevines, heavy with ripe, purple Concords. All of a sudden, we realized those grape vines were also heavy with raccoons. Those varmints were so crazy for grapes they weren't even afraid of us!" His voice rose to a peak. "We grabbed 'em by the scruff of their necks and flung 'em to the ground. They just climbed back up and continued gorging themselves!"

He told me to raise my trap a foot off the ground (raccoons will climb, skunks won't) and with grapes I'd catch raccoons every time. Sure enough, I had one the next morning and one or two every morning thereafter. I won't tell you what I did with 'em, but, except for the price of gas, it was tempting to take 'em over to New Hampshire across the river.

One morning I approached my trap expecting to see the usual grayish mass crouched in the corner. This morning, however, it looked different from a distance. It seemed lighter, almost red. When I reached the trap it was, indeed, different. There lay a nice, red fox, full of grapes and not at all nervous like a raccoon. He looked at me as if to say, "Okay, so I screwed up. Let me out!" I called Gil and he came right up. Gil was angry that his foolproof system had failed. We stood and admired Reddy Fox a few minutes before pouring him out of the trap and then watching him slink away into the late summer goldenrod. Gil said something about "popping him" if he dared do that again.

Then next morning he was back! I hoped Gil wouldn't "pop" him. What that fox obviously lacked in intellect, he made up for in sleekness and color. When Gil arrived, he just stood shaking his head. As we discussed the fox's fate, it occurred to me that Gil and I had previously joked about the New Hampshire caper. I think it came to both of us at the same time—he looked at me with a sparkle in his eyes and said he'd spring for the gas. We loaded Reddy Fox into the pickup and headed east so the world's stupidest fox could perpetuate his strain in a place away from Vermont, across the river in New Hampshire. ❧

Elm Planks with an Attitude

The other day my young friend, Walter, asked if I knew of a good place to swim. I mentioned the usual places—Curtis Pond, Putnamville Potholes or Shady Hill, before I remembered our own pond down in the pasture. Thoughts of that little pond and its contribution to my youth suddenly came swimming back. I could still feel the water's mixed messages of frigidness and July ecstasy as I talked. "Maybe it's still swimmable," I said. "If it is, you can

Stately Elm tree that frames the Morse Farm in East Montpelier. Elms made wonderfully strong planks.

Bernard Morse, thinking about swimming on a hot summer day, circa 1940.

skinny-dip there."

The pond was fed by an ancient brick-lined spring, nestled against an earthen bank at the water's edge. A long forgotten pipe led underground, away from the spring. It used to serve a valley farmhouse before an artesian well solved a modern need. A non-stop stream still rushes into the pond from the spring's two inch overflow pipe. It's the coldest water south of Hudson Bay and is so clean that even the smallest pebble shines through eight feet of azure translucence from the pond's bottom.

We had some great times down there. We rowed miles in an old rowboat that really had nowhere to go. There were fish, too. Because of that cold, oxidating overflow, the water was perfect for hundreds of nervous brookies (brook trout). Sometimes we'd catch them with open safety pins suspended from willow branches. One time my father heard a neighbor boast of catching a whole milk pail full down there. After that, there were a lot fewer fish.

The best thing we did at the pond, however, was swim. Kids are built to swim. It was there that our dog paddle beginnings broadened into variations of breaststroke and freestyle. It was there, also, that we began to notice girls were something more than a minor annoyance; at the pond we flirted with both maturity and girls.

My father built us a diving board one time. He bolted together two elm planks—said elm was "downright ornery," and would give us a hell of a spring. He pounded in two cedar posts just out from shore and spiked a crosspiece between them. The crosspiece supported the planks at a point toward their middle. He completed the job by dropping a boulder on the inland end of the planks with his bulldozer. Between the orneriness of the elm planks and father's well-planned pivot and fulcrum design, that board had a kick that sent us halfway across the pond. I can still see folks lined up, big and small, waiting for a chance at that great diving board!

We eventually outgrew the pond and went our separate ways. Ponds, like anything else, need a little TLC to thrive. Waterweeds sprouted like whiskers around its edges and it laid still, as if in mourning for the kids who no longer came. The old diving board stood guard for years and, in fact, had a life after the kids.

About the time we abandoned the old pond, my father sold his dairy cows and started raising vegetables for a living. He grew root crops and greens down in a field by the pond. Never one for convention, my father had a plan for washing those vegetables that employed both Yankee ingenuity and the old diving board. He put the vegetables into two steel egg baskets with ropes attached to their bales. Then he walked out to the end of the diving board with a basket dangling from each hand and proceeded to bounce. With every bounce, the baskets splashed into the cold, clear water and rose into the fresh air to drain. His operatic voice echoed through the fields, providing rhythm to the process—"Jerrrrusalem, Jerrrrusalem…" Five minutes of bouncing rendered those vegetables free of grit and ready for the cooking pot, guaranteed.

The old diving board finally dropped off its bearings. Beavers have since claimed it. There was not an Olympic swimmer among us, but we sure did have fun. I've lost track

Camp Comfort on Curtis Pond, a "rowing paradise," Maple Corner, Vermont.

of all those guys. Some of them may have good jobs and swimming pools in their back-yards. I wonder if they think of the old pond and the elm diving board as often as I do. As for myself—I'm still here on the same farm within walking distance of the old pond, but I don't go there often. I buy my beet greens somewhere else these days. They taste good, but they're full of grit. I guess some farmer did a poor job of washing 'em. 🍁

Space Age Cows

"Vermont farmer installs robot milking machines." That's the headline the other day that caught my eye. Heck no, it reached out, grabbed my tender psyche and rudely yanked it back to 1958. I was a pudgy ten-year-old sitting on a dock up at Woodbury Lake. The family reunion was in full swing and all of a sudden my father said we had to leave—had chores to do. "Cows don't take Sundays off," he said, as I begrudgingly joined my three older siblings and the family dog in the back seat of our '55 Plymouth. "Why can't we skip it today?" I whined, drawing only impatience from my three siblings. My father explained how our milk check put food on the table and paid our bills. "Milking's as important as family reunions to us," he said. Somewhere in the dissertation he used the word, "economy." We rode the rest of the way in silence. That word, "economy," clung in the air like a rainy day, obviously something important, but very annoying all at the same time. My watch said 4:05 when we pulled in the yard. Chore time. Thoughts of the family reunion faded as I got into my smelly barn clothes. We had sixty cows to milk.

My sister, Susie, and I went to get the cows from the pasture. Father stayed back at the barn to prepare the milking machines. We headed out the lane, a thoroughfare for cows formed by two parallel fences. At the end of the lane, the fences diverged into a wide-open day pasture, a huge area laced with cow paths and buttercups. We found the critters at a ledgy spot by our pond. "Cm'boss, cm'boss," I hollered, my tiny voice instantly attracting 120 big brown eyes. The critters, all but Althea, the furthest one away, gravitated in my direction. Susie walked way out to Althea and slapped her on the rump. Cows have different personalities. Althea was the herd malingerer, always was, always would be. We guided them back into the lane and through the big double doors at the end of our milking stable.

Ours was a modern barn for those times. It had two rows of stanchions going the barn's length and a broad walkway between those rows. A gutter ran on both sides of the walkway to catch everything non-milk from a cow. Above each stanchion, a fly-stained plaque bore names and lineage. Each cow had its own personal stanchion, claimed it religiously, and stood fidgeting for grain. Our milking machines were of two different brands and personalities, probably because father got a deal buying them that way—economy, again. The De Laval sat on the floor, with hoses and teat cups that went to the cow's udders. Cows actually "wore" the Surge via a thick leather belly belt that left the machine dangling from their middle. Putting the wrong machine on the wrong cow usually brought out cow wrath, sometimes spoken with a swift kick to the cerebral portion of the herdsman. We learned quickly from the cows.

Most cows savored chore time. It was their chance to relax, munch grain by the scoopful and spend a few quality minutes being pampered. We put them in the mood by massaging their udders with a warm, moist rag. Our fingers simulated the sucking motion of a calf. We talked to them, usually in kind, gentle tones. Every herd, however, has a misfit. Our misfit's name was Elsyni. She never warmed up to the human things that pleased most cows. She was a brindled mixture of Jersey and Ayrshire with a dash of Angus beef thrown in, a combination at odds with even minimal civility. God only knows why my father kept her around, but I remember Elsyni being at the Morse Farm for years, terrorizing all who milked her. In fact, that's when I first became a praying person. (Please God, don't let Elsyni kill me today). Elsyni stood Number 23 in the milking lineup. Everything on her sign was crossed out in favor of the hand-scribbled word "bitch." One time I approached Elsyni with her machine, the De Laval, well prepared to counter her terrorism with my practiced bobbing and weaving. That morning, however, she beat me to the draw. Before I even got to her side, she caught me with a well-placed left hoof to the head. The next thing I knew I was seeing stars and picking myself out of the gutter, half submerged in everything non–milk from a cow.

I think Elsyni finally ended up in someone's freezer and I'm still here at fifty-seven, a survivor. I don't care to milk cows anymore, but rest thankful there are folks who do. Today's dairy farmers are survivors of the highest order. No doubt, they all have an "Elsyni" story of their own they somehow lived to laugh about. I think toward the future and wonder about the relationship between robots and cows. Will those human hands, made huge through generations of milking, now shrivel to accommodate keyboards? How pleased will cows be by high-tech fingers and electronic words? Nobody knows the future, but I don't fault the modern farmer, no sir. He takes his cues from a thing called economy. 🍁

Houdini Returns

(Jackie Tollmann Photo)

"Gnome in Maple Burl."

A month ago, goats seemed like a good idea. We got them for the enjoyment of families who come to our store. There's nothing cuter or more personable than a goat. We have three kids, two nannies, and one old billy-goat. Some of them are Nubians, the ones with ears that lop over. Nubians win the cute award, hooves down. It all turned bad, though, when they started appearing in our store and helping themselves to the inventory. At first we wrote it off as cute, took them back to the enclosure, and added a few more planks. My brother, Elliott is the animal person around here—and the optimist. He said we finally had 'em licked. Within ten minutes, two of them were back in the store. Although the fence stood taller than us, we needed more. We bought chicken wire and Elliott stapled it between the planks. He was still laughing when he related this bit of staple slapstick:

"I had a plastic bagful of staples. All of a sudden that white nanny approached from the back and snatched it right out'a my hand. I looked around and she was grinnin'—SHE WAS GRINNIN'! I went for it. She backed up a step and shook it furiously. I was a whole hour pickin' those staples up!"

Soon the biggest Nubian appeared back at the store. This time it was far from cute, even to Elliott, but we were slowly making progress. Our fencing had finally impressed all, but this one maverick. I angrily grabbed her collar and yanked her back to the enclosure, returning her with a swift pat on the backside. Quicker than the shake of a goat's tail, she bounded over the six-foot fence and was again on the outside. I was beating my head against the fence and making muffled choking sounds when a father and daughter approached. As I pulled myself together and explained my exasperation, the errant goat went to father and daughter with a devilish grin and began pulling on their clothes. One more time I heard that awful word, "cute!"

I think I've figured out why goats can't be confined. They have an ancient homing instinct that triggers a need to return to the Alps (sort of the reverse of the Trapp Family story—"oh lady, oh who, who"). Due to a very small brain they usually get as far as the nearest geranium before their homing instinct deflates. Each return to captivity, however, re-activates the Alpine urge. Having figured this out, I was determined to find a better way of containing goats. Fences make great neighbors, but don't do squat for goats! I took my goat frustrations to the streets of Montpelier where I'm a Saturday morning vendor at the local farmers' market. As people approached my popcorn stand, I polled them on the subject. Most folks just stared blankly and quickly moved on. I did, however, get a couple suggestions worthy of note.

One guy said he once had an alcoholic goat—said four 16 oz. Budweisers might dull my goat's motor skills so it couldn't navigate the fence. "Humm, not bad," I thought. The other guy was a Vermonter thru and thru. He'd had reasonable luck keeping 'em in a '56 Pontiac. His system only failed when someone shot out the windshield. I really appreciated those ideas, but having no desire to confront the SPCA or start a junkyard, I dejectedly came home to the same old goat problem.

As I drove in the yard, Elliott was just dragging the puzzled Nubian back to the enclosure one more time. Like a defeated soldier, I joined him. We'd long since run out of planks and were down to miscellaneous tree branches and log slabs. By rote, we tacked more pitiful pieces to our disdained fence. Elliott, finally defeated, looked over his shoulder and muttered. "We'd be all right if it weren't for that EVIL thing over there!" His voice cracked and he pointed to the maverick Nubian.

We finally opted for the "have-a-heart" solution. We put the thing in our van and took it to some unsuspecting farmers in the next town. It may well end up the guest of honor at a goat-ka-bob. At the very least, I suspect it'll be confined to a barn in a locked stall and I really don't care. We're now getting along quite well with our remaining goats. I do, however, find myself looking around occasionally, expecting to see that Nubian heading east toward the Alps. ❦

Life in the "Slow" Lane

Sometimes I feel like the stupidest person in the world. Well—sometimes I am the stupidest person in the world! Early mornings are when I get stupid. It's usually friend bladder that wakes me up and friend coffee that finishes the job (Yes, I have two friends!). If those two guys work together with no glitches I'm usually upright and alright within an hour, but that wasn't the case last Thursday.

After I stumbled through friend bladder's message I lay on my bed with friend coffee and stared at all the friendly knots on my roughhewn ceiling. I see things in those knots; a wild stallion, assorted faces of people and animals, an airplane, maple leaves. I'M OKAY, REALLY. After a fashion, friend coffee nudged me closer to civility and I reached in my top drawer for a shirt. I grabbed one that had "Vermont" written colorfully across the front, put it on and struggled to the mirror.

My wife says I have to shave certain places on my face, even though I've had a beard since Mrs. Kreis sent me home from seventh grade with one word—Shave! As I gave lip service to the errant stubble, I noticed the seams of my T-shirt

looked coarse and ragged, like the shirt was on inside out, but the "Vermont" read just fine. "Brilliant," I thought, thinking I had proved the seams were just weird. I went to work, feeling pretty good. I was only at work a few minutes when one of my employees timidly told me the shirt was inside out. "IT IS NOT," I boomed defensively; then I realized I was at the mirror when "Vermont" read just fine. Embarrassed and feeling, yes, stupid, I hurried to the men's room.

My father was stupid once in the middle of the day. It was a few days before Halloween, and we needed some pumpkins to supplement our meager crop. He and my mother jumped in the pickup truck and headed for Malletts Bay where the lake-effect rain favors big, orange pumpkins. After comparing notes with the farmer about the weather and what it takes to grow the perfect pumpkin, they put on a heaping load and headed back down Malletts Bay Avenue toward Winooski. My father took a shortcut, up a steep street in a residential section. As they neared the top they were jarred by a sudden thump, like the slamming of a tailgate. A quick look in the rear view mirror confirmed what I'm sure my father already knew—he had not latched the tailgate and it had slammed open. Down that hill rolled a whole regiment of pumpkins, like a happy invasion of Normandy. My father said word passed through the neighborhood quick as a flash and kids began leaping from every house. He feared quick and total defeat by these tattered urchins from Winooski's seedy side. But my father misjudged the "seedy side" of Winooski.

"They scooped up pumpkins left and right," he said. "Some carried pumpkins as big as themselves but, by gosh, they didn't go back in the houses or behind the bushes like I expected. They trudged up to the truck and placed 'em in the bed. Before long they had replaced the whole load except for a few broken ones!" My father thanked them profusely and gave them each a pumpkin before he double checked the tailgate and headed home, feeling much smarter.

I continue to hope we all get smarter as life goes on. I think my father learned to always double check the tailgate and that round things'll roll every time, if given the chance. I learned that if your seams look coarse and tattered, your shirt's probably inside out and that mirrors never lie, they just communicate, well, inside out. The most important lesson is, however, to never, ever judge a book by its cover. I hope those kids from Winooski all went on to rich and rewarding lives because they were the salt of the earth. 🍁

Pumpkins for sale—Morse Farm, East Montpelier, Vermont.

Bus Season

Recently we took a deep breath, plunged into the depths of "bus season," and have yet to come up for air. Don't get me wrong. I'm not complaining. Bus season is good to us here at Morse Farm. Bus season is when tourists come to our place to learn about maple sugarin'. Yes, business is good, especially in light of our approaching winter, but meeting interesting folks from all over the world is what really turns me on about bus season. Here are two of my favorites:

United Kingdom: I especially love folks from the UK probably because my families, both Morse and Aiken, hail from there. The most memorable one this year was an elderly, robust gent. He approached me with the personality of a wrecking ball, his entire presence just inches from my face.

"We don't use much syrup back in the UKie (rhymes with pie). In fact we only use it on Pankike Die (Pancake Day)." When I pressed him about the nature of Pancake Day, he said it was some kind of religious holiday. Our conversation led to more interesting tidbits about life in England and it was soon time for him to go. Just before he left, obviously thinking of my need to sell maple syrup, he nudged a little closer and shouted, "Ye should 'ave a Pankike Die in America, Gov'nah." With that he elbowed me painfully in the ribs and walked off with a deep, self-satisfied grumble. I thought to myself, "Pancake Day, indeed! We eat pancakes every day in America."

America's South: Another favorite was a fellow from the Southern part of our country. He sidetracked me after my sugarhouse presentation to talk about the cane syrup process in the South. He reminisced of mules walking in circles to grind the cane and kids getting into the juice before it was boiled. That had all been told to me before, but one thing he said about "cat-head biscuits" stopped me short. He went on to describe the heavenly taste of fresh cane syrup poured over a cat-head biscuit. Visions of head cheese and other products made from the cerebral end of animals lingered in my mind. He sensed my puzzlement and came to my rescue before I had to ask the stupid question. "Have no feah, suh," he said in his perfect Jimmy Carterese, "I'm talkin' about the sahz of the biscuits, not the content." After that, I was much better able to imagine those biscuits with butter melting into the hot syrup...ummmm good!

We get bus loads of Amish, Aussies and Auklandites. Sometimes buses even break down in our yard and we host passengers for hours while they wait. One time I saved the day for a driver of one of those foreign made buses. He needed a special fan belt that was not available in any of our local parts stores. We were about to give up the search when I found that the belt on our John Deere lawn tractor was a perfect fit!

There's never a boring day in bus season. 🍁

Maple Peace

These days I'm talking to folks who come to see our foliage from all over the world; you might call it a "well rounded" sales approach. First we herd them into our sugarhouse and tell them about the brief sugar season. We describe the mud and snow and the grueling work of gathering sap. When we say it takes forty gallons of sap to make one gallon of maple syrup, they're ready to call in the Red Cross. There's no better way to market something than with the truth mixed with a touch of good, honest "local color." I recently

Not a still—just looks like one! Sidney Morse makes maple syrup outdoors.

heard a term for what we do. It's called "agritainment." Agritainment goes both ways—they learn from me; I learn from them.

Take Midwesterners, for instance. Midwesterners are great fun—a little reserved with their laughter, but great fun. Their accents, to my ears, are a pleasant marriage between mild Southern and Yankee (other than the northern tier). There the Scandinavian influence is as broad as amber waves of grain, yaw. They call corn-on-the-cob "roastin' ears," and they don't want to be told their land is flat. There are places in the Midwest where the countryside is rolling and Midwesterners are as proud of their hills as Maria Von Trapp was of the highest pinnacle. One guy from Kansas told me they measure land out there in square sections. I said we measure land in small patches between ledges. He laughed and then accepted my square deal.

Folks from West Virginia are a lot like native Vermonters except the way they talk. I joked to one guy about making something besides maple syrup in our sugarhouse at night. He said his "daddy" used to make it and he could tell me how —"You gotta use coppah stee-ils to make the best whought loughtnin'." When he finished, I felt qualified for a whole new enterprise.

We get lots of international groups, too. I've heard many different dialects and must admit, like the grades of maple syrup, the flavors are very different. Folks from Israel speak with a serious dialect that projects persistence and strength. They are here to learn. Israeli children always sit quietly with rapt attention. The Russians communicate with their deep Russian eyes, but speak a dialect that leaves out words like "the." (Why we need stupid little word, anyway?)

I especially like the Dutch dialect. Dutch talk lilts. It's animated. It's a veritable caricature of a dialect. "Vee take der highveigh down from Hardvik. Der color iss vonderful!" No wonder Holland is such a peaceful country. Who could make war with people who talk like that?

The folks I feel most akin to, however, are the English, probably because I am. I tell them that I came from their neck of the woods a while back, from Dedham, Essex County, in 1635. They giggle and say I'm looking good. I've never been called a bloke or a chap by a single Englishman; they don't do that. Instead, they use "alright" (pronounced "ahwroigt") as a casual greeting and "brilliant" as a common observation. They're extremely polite, always thanking you when they make the payment and again when they accept the change.

The most baffling dialect, however, comes from the Scotsmen. Yesterday a guy approached me with a question.

"Dis yor shahgger tame coom ah th' lost und ah woontah?" (Does your sugar time come at the last end of winter?) "Sorry," I pointed to myself, raised my voice a level, and spoke slowly, "I…speak…English."

"Tis," he said. "Where are you from?" I asked, trying to be polite.

"Scootland" he said.

"Oh," I replied. "Is it your first time in America?"

"Iye."

"Do you like it here?"

"Iye."

I explained that sugaring does come at the end of winter and we parted with a handshake, a dialect more common.

Speaking of language and dialect, I think maple syrup speaks universally, like a handshake. My grandfather was a United States Senator for thirty-three years and sat on the Foreign Relations Committee. He traveled widely and met leaders from all over the world. He'd give a quart of Vermont maple syrup to those who were "up to no good"—said it tamed them down immediately. I can believe that. Somehow I doubt there's anyone in Congress these days using that kind of diplomacy. I think they should. Maple syrup speaks. Iye. 🍁

Signs of the Times

We had an unusual fall this year. My father always forecasted a foliage peak on or around his birthday, October 3. This year, however, Mother Nature had different plans. I waited through the first week of October, declared foliage 2004 a wash, and started apologizing to all the folks who arrived to see it. Then on October 12, as silently as a mouse, it came in the night with a quality that left mouths agape and cameras clicking. I never saw a more spectacular presentation from friend Autumn who has truly never let me down in fifty-six seasons.

Today my wife is raking the aftermath of foliage 2004 off our lawn and I'm okay with it. The best show always "leaves 'em wanting more."

But wait a minute. We're not done with autumn colors yet. Vibrant colors are springing up all over again, this time from the ground up. Like the leaves, these colors are temporary, helpful to the economy, and draw lots of attention. I'm talking about the signs, those cussed political signs, that have taken over our lawns (not mine) and intersections like wild mushrooms, the bad kind. Of course, I'm glad for the printers and graphic designers, but what in this world could those things possibly have to do with anyone's qualifications to hold public office? In fact, I'm so sick of 'em right now the only one I can support is Coldwell Bankers.

This minor tantrum led me east the other day toward New Hampshire. I had to get away. I drove Route 302 past East Barre and Groton through a rainy mishmash of balding Vermont hills and more signs. I stopped at the P&H Truck Stop, sat between two truckers and ordered precisely what the doctor didn't — eggs over easy, sausage and home fries. When the tired looking waitress brought my fare I ate, hungrily, feeling the weight shift from my shoulders to my stomach. A final slurp of strong coffee led me to the cashier and out into the yard. I wished I could get into an eighteen wheel Freightliner instead of my puny Nissan. Route 302 east of the Connecticut River and Route 3 in the White Mountains quickly proved that political signs have no borders. I popped in a JJ Johnson CD, which

(Jackie Tollmann Photo)

"Grandma Nellie."

fueled me, happier, to Franconia Notch. I stopped briefly at the Old Man of the Mountain but didn't get out of the car—he was now just a memory.

As I continued past Cannon Mountain and the Flume, a sudden homing instinct struck the Nissan and me at the same time. I turned north on I-93, ignoring exits that promised more fun in the White Mountains. Crossing Moore Reservoir and back into The Green Mountain State, I felt my mood lightening. Rolling hills to the west were highlighted by, yes, sunshine. I reached to turn off the wipers and soon pulled into the new Waterford Welcome Center. A pleasant lady greeted me from behind a brochure-clad counter. We discussed the sudden weather change and the brilliance of our recent foliage season. The friendliness of the place impressed me. I returned to my car feeling healthy, like the environment around me.

Pleased with my new mental state I continued toward home, choosing Route 15 west of West Danville. I stopped at Rowell's Sugarhouse and Buck's Furniture, two places I had always wanted to stop, finding friendly folks in both. The political signs somehow seemed less offensive as I traveled the final leg of my journey. They brought to mind that Dr. Seuss story about the "Star-Belly Sneetches"— some have "stars upon thars" and others don't. I chuckled to myself with the sweet revelation that people, like Sneetches, need to express who they are and how they feel. Right now they're using signs on their lawns instead of stars on their bellies. I drove in my yard rejuvenated and comfortable that Election Day this year will soon come and go like the autumn leaves. 🍁

Gimpy Goblin

Halloween's comin'! Halloween, to me, is more than just a night of dress up and hell raisin'. Searching my "nostalgia library," I find a pudgy Burr Morse gazing through school windows at autumn's brilliance. An aching urge to go jump in leaves or at least walk through the woods, finds me counting the days. Halloween is the first break in that annoyance that starts in September and seems to go on forever. It is the beginning of three exciting holidays that bring dreams and surprises.

My parents had energy for holidays and one particular Halloween stands out as extra special. They planned a haunted house for the whole neighborhood and much creativity went into it. There were to be swooping things in the trees that lighted and came alive at strategic times and "feely" things like fresh liver to simulate brains. My father's role on the big night would be to dress in Grandma Morse's old buffalo robe. The robe had been in storage since the days when it was used to keep Grandma and her sisters warm on January sleigh rides. It would serve as a perfect exterior for a snapping, snarling monster who would greet kids exiting from the tunnel fashioned from hoops made of maple branches and the big farm truck canvas. To us it was as long and curving as a dragon's innards and lots more fun.

I remember the excitement of those preparations as if it were yesterday, and the waiting was almost unbearable. Finally, Halloween night arrived with the appearance of assorted ghosts, goblins and rubber-faced Eisenhowers. We were quickly grabbed by ghoulish staffers and escorted to a place where everything that dangles, moans, blats or crawls lived. There, fun and fear competed for our youthful attention and scariest of all was that dark, snarling monster at the end of the tunnel. My father brought that old buffalo robe to life as he sent everyone but a bold Martha Holden running for their lives—Martha grabbed a nearby stick and whacked the monster a good one right in the head!

Dad walked around with a major egg on his head for a few days. Martha apologized with the disclaimer, "How was I supposed to know that thing was a person?" Talk of the occasion went on for weeks afterward. Those most special times in life were always a little better the second time around on a date with nostalgia, something we have plenty of here in Vermont. 🍁

Deer Season

This fall, a female visitor asked me what my summer name was. "Huh?" I said. Well, she figured "Burrrrr" was my winter name, so I ought to have a summer name. I just laughed it off, but, you know, maybe it wasn't such a bad idea.

Nature presents us with neurotic weather changes, weasels and hares change their colors two times a year, and then those chameleons. Wait a minute, between the fickleness of nature and our four-legged friends, maybe we humans are the stable ones around here and should leave it well enough alone.

We've already had twelve inches of snow and thirty-six-inch drifts, followed by melting and heavy rains. Right now, there's water everywhere. People are walking around stunned with the flip-flops of this season between fall and winter. What do we call this time of year, "Finter?" Until someone comes up with something better, I'll stick with tradition: It's "Deer Season" here in Vermont!

(David Aiken Photo)

That's "Deer" season, although hunters best include "Dear" in their vernacular. Our divorce rate always spikes in Deer Season. Take my chain-saw repair guy, for instance. Steve is a brute of a man. His ruddy, bewhiskered face rests midway between a well-worn Husqvarna cap and barn-wide shoulders. He sits, no, he crouches, on a stool behind his service counter shouting phrases like, "NEVER GUESS AT THE OIL MIX FOR A CHAINSAW!!" and, "WHO THE HELL WAS THE LAST ONE TO RUN THIS SAW!!?" I was in there today after struggling for days to find him open. He's a deer hunter.

"Got your deer yet, Steve?" I asked. "Hell no! Only saw two spike horn and a four pointer so far", he said, quieter than his chainsaw voice.

"Why didn't you drop the first one you saw? (hunters don't "shoot" deer, they "drop'em"), I asked.

"I can't take one that early in the season unless it's got a big rack," he continued with an obscene level of confidence. "There's three more days of huntin'. I'll wait for a better 'un—If I get mine too early, I've done myself outta the rest a'the season. Ya see, I love t'hunt." He didn't really need to tell me that.

I'm not a hunter. It's a little embarrassing, seven generation Vermonter like I am, but I gotta be honest.

My father took me out one time when I was a teenager. He naturally assumed I had hunting in my blood. We drove up County Road and he dropped me off, armed with an old 30-30 rifle, a little south of Maple Corner. My instructions were to meet him at the Martin Place, an abandoned settlement, somewhere in the woods between Robinson Hill and Worcester Village. He said he'd stop at the Maple Corner Store, buy lunch for us and join me from a different direction.

I timidly cradled the 30-30 and headed in the direction he pointed. Back then knowledge of shooting was limited more to one's genetics than any formal training. I trudged along wondering what I would do if I actually saw a deer. My fears compounded with every step; I felt lost. I was hungry. I remembered shuffling through the leaf mold and deliberately stepping on dead limbs, comforted that my noise might help someone find me. It seemed like I had been walking forever when I blundered up a rise onto a level area where new growth hard woods mingled with scrub apple trees. It had the markings of an abandoned homestead. I stopped to catch my breath, proud that I had actually found the settlement. A gentle tap on my shoulder made me nearly jump out of my skin! My father stood behind me, looking more amused than anything else. "I heard you comin' a mile away. You sounded like a herd of elephants!" he said in a soft hunter's voice. He beckoned me over to an old cellar-hole where a brown bag held our lunch. We sat on the rocks and ate cheddar cheese and hard rolls. It was the best lunch I ever had. 🍁

The Night Blooming Cereus

Dot Morse socializing with her Cereus.

The other day I was down at my mother's house visiting and she was quite excited. Her Night Blooming Cereus was sending long tendrils out into her kitchen. They were taking over the place, "Little Shop of Horrors" style. You might think a ninety-year-old woman would be scared of such a thing, but she considered it entertainment—said the plant was just "acting out" a little, much like the Morse family's Cereus ancestor did forty-five years earlier.

I was a small boy in a Vermont farm family. We had no TV and, well, between barn chores and field work there wasn't time for TV anyway. Once a year my mother's Night Blooming Cereus begot a blossom of biblical aroma and brilliance. It was as big around as a dinner plate and provided one of our family's most important social events of the whole year. The darned Cereus had a mind of its own, however. It announced its intentions to blossom only hours before the event and that blessed blossom only lived for a couple of hours. On "bloom" night my mother invited folks from the neighborhood, boiled up some hot-spiced cider and popped some corn. We all sat and talked, our eyes fixed on that big prehistoric-looking bud. There were lots of different personalities in the room, but the most memorable was old Hazel Frisk with her nervous cackling. "Dot, that Cereus better bloom soon or it'll be time for morning chores, hackle, hackle, hackle, puck, puck!" Around 9:00 PM, someone exclaimed and before our eyes, that brilliant white starburst was unhinged. The Cereus put on a fantastic show for everyone in the room.

One time, my grandmother, Mildred Morse, invited the neighbors in for a "Cereus" show. On the guest list were Dr. and Mrs. Cherrington, the Boston socialites who bought our ancestral farm in Maple Corner. There were more than a few people that night, possibly because of Mildred's reputation for great tasting pastries. My grandparents had just moved to the new farm and my grandfather, Sidney, had things unrelated to the floral kingdom on his mind. He had just installed a new gutter cleaner in the barn and couldn't wait to show it to the men. The men trooped off, including the bow-tied Harvard professor, to inspect the inner workings of manure handling. They never did make it back for the evening's main event. We sure knew how to have a good time back then!

My mother's Cereus bloomed about a month ago to far less fanfare than back in the old days, but times, they change. Some of the "entertainment" these days is far worse than the Cereus—think of that horrid halftime show at the 2004 Super Bowl! I'll say one more time, when nature's driving, it's usually in a good direction. Bravo Night Blooming Cereus! Bravo! 🍁

Regal Wreaths

A couple of weeks ago I traveled to the Northeast Kingdom early one morning to visit Luc and Jacinthe Marchesseault. Jacinthe (pronounced JaSaint) had promised to make a balsam wreath for me to see. I was looking for a new wreath maker, but needed to see the product before I ordered. Working seven days a week all summer found me a bit "stir crazy," and the Northeast Kingdom, my favorite part of Vermont, beckoned as my restorer of sanity.

As my van wove north into the crisp, pre-autumn air, I thought of my grandfather, the late U.S. Senator George D. Aiken. Long ago he proclaimed in the U.S. Senate: "This small piece of God's country, this land of spectacular flora and fauna, deserves a noble ranking. I hereby declare it the Northeast Kingdom." The Kingdom stands to this day deserving in its nobility, but for one missing ingredient—money. It remains the most impoverished patch of earth east of the Mississippi and thoughts of adding to its coffers made me feel good.

The directions I had to Luc's Body Shop brought me nicely to my destination. I was greeted by a friendly French barking dog. Answering my first knock, an expectant Luc and Jacinthe showed me into their living room where the most beautiful Christmas wreath I had ever seen lay on the table. After proper exclamations and a quick order, Luc (pronounced Luke) asked if I wanted to see his Christmas trees. We loaded into his aging pickup and headed out back of the

Senator Aiken with Dot and Harry Morse at Morse Farm in East Montpelier.

body shop into his tree plantation.

"You like them tree," he spoke, in more of a statement than a question. We rattled on past rows and rows of beautifully manicured trees and stepped out somewhere in the middle. Luc impulsively grabbed his ax from the back and walked proudly to one of the better ones. "I sell them tree to highess bidder," he said, matter of factly. "Nobody gonna steal them tree or I with this hax, chase them off my propertee!"

I nodded in agreement. It is so much work to grow perfect Christmas trees and his were perfect. Looking out over the green rows that went on to merge with the rest of God's country, I felt much wiser for the visit that day. Not only had I found "the perfect wreath," but I made new friends. I was now connected to a special nobility in a kingdom where wealth was measured by hard work, natural beauty, and knowing more than one language. 🍁

Tessa and the Spice of Life

My old Beagle Tessa passed away the other day. Tessa was one of my best friends. I first met her on a snowy day some fifteen years ago. She was born an only Beagle child, to parents of proven disposition and grace. You see, I had a problem with dogs. My dog experience had been flavored by a love affair with Nipper, the dog of my youth. Nipper was a black Beagle with a white necktie and he went away to Heaven when I was in my late teens. His death left little room for anymore "dog love" in my heart. My wish, post-Nipper, was to enjoy the canine community from a distance and I succeeded for twenty years. When my sons reached the ages of ten and eight, they wanted a dog as young boys will. Being a good father, I relented, but with one selfish stipulation: the new dog must be a Beagle, a black Beagle with a white necktie.

We visited Tessa one fall day. She had just been born and needed to stay with her mother a few more weeks. Her owner, a man whom Betsy worked with, took us to a pen in his garage. The mother lay at the front of the pen, happy to see us. The man reached deep into an old blanket and gently pulled our Tessa out, said she had a peculiar habit of burrowing. He handed her to Betsy and as we huddled, we knew our family had just grown by one.

We counted the minutes until one day, four weeks later, the man called and said Tessa was ready to come with us. She settled in like a pat of butter on a hot stack of pancakes. The boys were instantly ecstatic. Betsy reserved judgment until after the housebreaking process and I kind of stayed at arm's length. Could this devilish little thing possibly fill the huge void left by Nipper so long ago? As time went on, Tessa grew, fat, to lanky, to fat again. As dogs will do, she sniffed out the family "hard-sell," and that's where she dedicated her diplomacy. She took to my bed, above all the others, and burrowed deep down into the bedding every night. I got hooked on her warmth. I expected Tessa's burrowing would have sealed our bond on its own, but she carried it one step further, just to make sure. She showed

Robinson Morse with
Spice and Tessa.

me she loved my jazz. Tessa was very undog-like in the matter of music. You see, she never left or howled disagreement with the high pitches when I played jazz trombone in my music room. Instead, she lay on the rug at the base of my stool and savored every phrase. She accepted my mistakes with patience and allowed me to stretch to foolish levels. Tessa clearly loved jazz. Together, we grew musically and otherwise—our bond was complete.

The boys grew up and moved on and Tessa had been an old dog for a while now. Recently, my mother-in-law moved in to our home, bringing with her Spice, a young Springer Spaniel. To me, a one Beagle man, Spice was a little hard to take from the start. We set some strict ground rules, Tessa and me:

1. *The bed, and especially burrowing, is off limits.*
2. *The music room is off limits (no problem at all for Spice, she hates my jazz).*
3. *Keep back a dog's length and we'll get along okay.*

We were able to live nicely with the ground rules for a while but, alas, Tessa recently started to fail. She had a terrible night on Monday and passed away at 1:30

Tuesday afternoon. Betsy and I walked around like zombies afterward. We gathered ourselves enough to call the boys to tell them. Then we noticed we were not alone in our suffering. Spice was taking Tessa's death harder than anyone. She paced from door to door and was at loose ends all night. We were puzzled because Spice should not have known about Tessa's death. She didn't see it. As I emerged from sleep the next morning, there was a familiar warmth way down deep in the bedding. "What the…?" I mumbled, remembering my Tessa was gone. Spice had burrowed in sometime in the night. When I got up and relaxed into my morning sofa for coffee, Spice came and lay down against my feet. Tessa seemed to be communicating to Spice, "Look, this guy is hurting. Go comfort him." I felt Tessa's spirit—heck, I saw proof of it! I'm now glad to welcome Spice into my life since it's what Tessa wanted and this time it won't take twenty years. 🍁

The Balloon Lady

Last night I was on my way to a music practice in Burlington. As I headed out the door I heard a powerful "ffshchch," like a gas flame, but more powerful than the kitchen stove. Right off I knew it was the balloon lady who has been using our big hay field to take off from. The "ffshchch" was closer than it should have been, considering the take off point is a half-mile away. I quickly dropped my horn and hurried toward the noise, which was coming in scary frequency—she was obviously trying to gain altitude quickly. A short ways up into the woods, another "ffshchch" led my eyes to the brightly colored balloon hovering, perfectly framed by a hole in the canopy of red, golden and orange leaves.

"Hey, are you okay?" I hollered. "I'm fine—just fine," she shouted, and as the magnificent thing left the frame, I heard in smaller words…"I love you."

I knew she didn't mean it "that" way. She was just high on a special mixture of adrenaline and beauty, a thing called life at its best, and I was just there as a convenient sounding board. The wonder of it all lingered as I drove on to Burlington.

We're all flirting with this thing called life and it occurred to me one more time, if you're going to take the ride, you might as well love it. Three cheers, balloon lady. I love you, too. 🍁

Music for Better or Worse

Besides being a farmer, I'm a "home-grown" trombone player. I play at venues from jazz to classical. Keeps me sane, you know, at least as sane as I get these days.

Last week I held down the second trombone seat in a local chamber orchestra concert. We'd been practicing for a month and felt pretty good about it. We started the concert with Mozart's Overture to the Magic Flute and, if I say so myself, did noble justice to the opening chords. Our conductor's smile said it all.

Like weather in Vermont, however, the attitude of music can change instantly without notice. We had just started the Allegro theme that has some lovely soft places. Right at the softest point, a place brasses better be subdued or incur the wrath of whole neighborhoods, I did something for the first time in my life, totally involuntarily, mind you. I coughed into the mouthpiece of my instrument. Now, there's something about a cough zinging through umpteen feet of trombone tubing, projecting out the bell and into a massive concert hall that's, well, disconcerting. I was horrorstruck! I looked out over the heads of the woodwinds, past the second violins to our conductor. Her smile went from animato to agitato quite prestissimo! In fact, the striking "O" that formed on her mouth reminded me of that Edvard Munch painting, "The Scream."

I instantly went into damage control mode. I impulsively looked at my neighbors on either side to transfer the blame, like folks do when personal flatulence strikes. My trombone partners had beaten me to the punch, however. They were both braced, ninety degrees in my direction, with wide grins on their faces—I had been caught red-handed. It seemed the tone had been set for the rest of our evening. We never fully recovered from that moment of trombone trauma. We stayed ragged to the end, a detail skillfully reported by our local music critic in the next day's paper. We ended the evening with Schubert's Unfinished Symphony No. 8, only we finished it, just barely.

Our conductor was really quite forgiving, a prerequisite for a conductor of amateur musicians. We joked about it afterwards and I redeemed myself the next day by contributing to a stellar, second concert (How come those critics only attend the bad ones?). A good friend of mine, Carl, is a conductor of a local village band. He told a funny story once about a similar musical outburst.

He was at his first rehearsal with the group. As he looked out over the bevy of musicians, the tuba player caught his eye. The player was a little old man named Harold who had a cherubic grin and held the instrument like he was in love with it. My friend needed someone to play the tuning note and kindly asked Harold if he would. The old man first looked puzzled, and then placed the huge mouthpiece to his lips, heisted up off his chair, and blew as if his life depended on it. Out from that big toilet-shaped bell spewed a long disgusting blat, closer resembling an elephant fart than a concert B flat. "It was awful," my friend said. The first clarinet player quickly approached the conductor's podium and whispered, "Harold just likes to hold the horn, he doesn't really play it!" Carl said Harold settled back into his chair caressing the horn, obviously pleased with himself.

I'm proud to say my sons are both musicians. Folks mention it to me quite often and assume the boys got their musical talents from me. I always set the record straight and tell them the boys got their talents from my wife, Betsy. They remark that Betsy must be quite a musician, herself. "No," I say, "Betsy can't croak a note. She was once told by her choir director to just move her lips and never let any sound come out!" No, Betsy's no musician, but she's the one who made them practice. Betsy gave the boys their music. ❦

Deep Roots Back Home

We lit the first fire in our wood stove last night. In the morning I rose early enough to sit close to the stove with the black dog, Rumi, my son, Rob's companion. We snuggled, letting the stove's warmth course clear through to our bones. Although man and dog do not communicate in human terms, I had the distinct feeling that Rumi and I shared a common thought; home is a wonderful place to be.

It was with this notion that I rose early on November 1st, slurped a quick cup of coffee, and followed a little voice in my head that beckoned me clear to Medfield, Massachusetts where I would meet two distant cousins. Our ancestors settled the Dedham-Medfield area in 1635 and my cousins wanted to show me our roots. Our focus was on an archaeological dig at a cellar-hole, the possible home site of my seventh great-uncle, Lt. Samuel Morse. The homestead burned during King Philip's War during 1676. The archaeologists had been hired for a one day dig to verify if it was, indeed, Lt. Sam's place.

I met the cousins at the Medfield Historical Society and we drove, as if guided by a familial "On-Star System," to an oaken plot at the edge of town. Boston area traffic hummed nearby as we walked into the woods, still feeling guided. We found the site, some 150 yards from where we had parked and the same distance from several suburban houses. The archaeologists expected us and seemed glad to answer our questions. They showed us some ancient nails, two pieces of glass and a dark line that ran across the bottom of one of their plots. They said that indicated a burned timber. We were like kids on Christmas morning, anticipating proof positive quickly and painlessly. The professionals, however, remained noncommittal—said there was nothing yet to indicate it had been a Morse dwelling. They said the day's findings would be taken to a lab and we'd see a report in a few weeks. We thanked them and wandered off into the oaks, a little disappointed. Like dogs in the woods, we walked circuitously, stopping to examine stones and miscellaneous debris. We gathered at a ridge and speculated that it was probably the road to Lt. Sam's place back before Boston traffic.

After we left the cellar-hole site, we toured the oldest houses of Medfield and stopped at cemeteries where toppling headstones displayed fading names like Eliakim, Mehitable and Dorcas. The surname, "Morse," showed up at every stop. It was dark when we gathered by our cars to part. We all agreed the day had been superb and that no lab report was necessary for us—we knew the cellar-hole belonged to our ancestor. We'd felt it in our bones. On the long ride back to Vermont, I thought about creatures and their homing instincts. Memories of our black Beagle, Nipper, came to mind somewhere in Central New Hampshire.

My father always took Nipper along when he did errands. One time Dad took him on an errand run to Worcester, twelve miles away, let him out, and unintentionally drove home without him. Nipper was left to find his own way home. He went east over Ellis Hill towards County Road, the logical way. At the intersection with County Road, seven miles north of our place, Nipper encountered my Uncle Bernard. Bernard was operating a bulldozer at the time, and the two knew each other well. They exchanged pleasantries and a tired Nipper anxiously accepted Bernard's invitation to ride "shotgun" on the bulldozer for the rest of the day. After work Bernard delivered Nipper back home—a trip powered by homing instinct with a little help from some heavy equipment and a kind uncle!

I chuckled at the thought. Much like a dog, I had spent the day following my homing instinct. I had a great experience, did a little 'sniffing around,' and now I was on my way again. We creatures are all the same; we'll always get back home one way or another. 🍁

Animal Power Personified

Soon we'll be decorating our Christmas wreaths. Our cone supply lasts several years, but a recent inspection found that we were low. Yesterday, I called our family's ancestral farm's new owner, got permission to pick, and hopped in my van. Enroute, the thought occurred to me that I should have lined up some help. Picking cones is a little like picking strawberries, as my lower back now remembered, but I continued on anyway. The van climbed up Robinson Hill and stopped at the stand of Norway Spruce which now loomed over what once was our hay field. I got out and my wary bones carried the bundle of empty burlap bags out into the trees.

I was surprised at the darkness at that time of the afternoon. The trees were bigger and denser than I remembered. I had not gathered cones for several years. My eyes pitched downward. A part of me was hoping this was not a cone year, but I knew better. I bent down and began my gathering, aware that night would come quicker this first week back on Eastern Standard Time. My bag filled slowly; the squirrels overhead voicing their noisy objections. "Get out of my life, you little creeps," I thought. To a maple sugarmaker, squirrels have no redeeming qualities. I picked up a small stone, mostly because I needed a stretch, and hurled it toward the noise. It landed at the base of a distant Norway, highlighting a texture different from the surrounding forest floor. I walked over to investigate and lying on the ground were hundreds of cones, gathered into a well-organized cone yard. "Could it be," I thought? I looked up into the evergreens. The racket momentarily stopped as if to answer my question. Those squirrels had done the job of gathering—they were my helpers!

I dropped down, now scooping up cones with ease. There were also other cone yards I soon found. In no time, I completed the entire harvest. I carried the full bags back to the van, my bones now quite contented. For those who would charge me with robbing the poor squirrels' food supply, I am confident there is plenty left for them. Squirrels always take more than they need.

My good friend, Alden Belcher, grew up in Ontario. One of his early jobs was working for a man who raised both vegetables and pigs. One year they had a bumper crop of turnips and the farmer sent him out to turn the pigs into the turnip field for feeding. Alden got the pigs situated, but noticed they were having difficulty biting off chunks; round turnips are just the wrong shape for a pig's mouth. He tried cutting one in half with his jack knife and found that solved the problem. Alden got down on his knees and proceeded to prepare the whole field this way. After a period of time, he sensed that he was not working alone. He turned around and looked behind him. The pigs were hard at work, rolling turnips into piles with their snouts. They realized that Alden's job would be easier, not to mention their own gastronomical pleasure, if they gathered the turnips for him. Three cheers for the four-footed workforce! 🍁

South view of the Robinson Farm in Maple Corner.
Burr gathered cones close to where this picture was taken.

Gramp's Taxi

It's cross-country ski season again here at the Morse Farm Maple Sugarworks and we have a new grooming machine for our ski trails. It's called a Piston Bully and it's a wonderful machine. It's got a roto-tiller for chopping up ice, a special drag attachment that leaves an eight-foot swath smooth and perfect, and has another little gadget for making tracks on one side of the trail (skiers love their tracks). It also has a bulldozer blade which angles in any imaginable position, and lights, lots of lights. We can go just about anywhere, day or night, with our Piston Bully, and we do. About the only thing it can't do is make snow. Right now, we need snow so Mr. Bully can get out there and do his job. In fact, I've got his heater plugged in right now so he'll be ready. Oh, I forgot to tell you. For being such a versatile winter worker, Mr. Bully has one other limitation: he hates cold temperatures. We've got to plug him in hours before his Mercedes diesel engine will come to life.

When I was a boy, Leslie Hooper sold Studebakers around here. Leslie was a neighbor. He was forever showing up with the latest Hawks and Larks, but Dad

SNOWROLLERS—
Every so many years we have snowrollers.
Snowballs are created by the winds
and moisture in the snow.

never did buy. Our father was a Chevy man—said he wouldn't be caught dead driving something that sounded like it could also hatch eggs. Then one day, Leslie came with a different car, a new, dynamic product line, something that used a less expensive fuel and would last four times as long on our salty Vermont roads. It had a dignified name and very pleasant styling. My father was impressed with the new car, a Mercedes. It came clear from Germany and used diesel fuel instead of gasoline. Somehow I think we would have owned one of those cars, had it not been for the price. In spite of the Mercedes' fuel economy and longevity, it proved a hard sell to most frugal Vermonters.

Leslie finally did sell one to Gramp's Taxi. Gramp had a fleet of one and no last name that anyone knew about, a "singular" sort of guy. To him, the Mercedes offered the best of both worlds. He could carry his fares for half the fuel cost and would never have to buy another taxi. Life was good for Gramp after the Mercedes arrived in July, but problems began the first frosty morning in October. Diesels don't start well in cold weather, especially ones of that vintage. Gramp was mad and got madder with every new starter that poor Leslie had to deny warranty on. They went around and around, irate customer and frustrated salesperson. Finally, toward the end of the month, they reached a rather dubious solution: Gramp should start up the Mercedes and simply leave it running until sometime in April. And that is just what Gramp did!

He faithfully kept the thing topped off with fuel and learned to live with the situation except for one problem, personal rather than automotive: Gramp went out on a drinking binge about once a month. He'd be gone a few days, leaving his poor wife with the Mercedes in the yard, purring away. Leslie had warned them about letting the thing run out of fuel—"You'll never get a diesel started if it runs out of fuel," he said. The "Mrs." took that to heart, but suffered with a personal problem of her own. Neither she nor any of the neighbors knew how to turn the damned thing off! Older diesels respond to a "kill button" rather than a switch key when they respond at all. Sometimes, they just sit there making muffled "clacking" sounds in total defiance of the kill button. Mrs. Gramp was scared to death of the cussed thing. I guess it was poor Leslie's cross to bear, along with his meager commission, but he got a call from the Mrs. every time Gramp went out on a binge. "I'm so sorry to bother you again, Mr. Hooper, but Gramp is gone for a few days. Could you please come down and shut that car off?" Leslie would drop whatever he was doing, drive down to Montpelier and turn off Gramp's taxi.

Like Leslie said, the car lasted fifteen years. It served faithfully to old Gramp as long as he kept it running, literally. One day Gramp departed to the "big taxi stand in the sky." The Mercedes got sold to a man who drove it, but only in the summer, black soot now belching from its worn out bowels. Our area didn't "warm up" to diesels for a long time after that (neither did diesels warm up to our area, for that matter). Diesels start better these days except for our Piston Bully. Oh what the heck—I stay close to home in the winter and don't mind keeping it plugged in. ❧

The Snow Monster

Let it snow, let it snow, let it snow—seems to be the mantra of choice here in Central Vermont, normally a paradise for cross-country skiers. This year, though, our countryside's as barren as the Gobi Desert. Adding insult to injury, folks in places like Galveston Island, Texas are stealing our snow and even sharing it with Mexico. And one more mention of how much snow we used to get will put me right over the edge—although they're right, you know. We used to get more snow than you could shake a large shovel at. Heck, we'd lose whole villages under the darned stuff. That's one reason churches have steeples, I suppose, so there's something that'll stick up above the snow!

Way back when I was a boy we even had monsters to help with snow control. Ours was a picturesque farm, the last place on a peaceful country road in Calais. From our parlor window, the same one my grandmother looked out when she was a girl, we could see everyone who approached. Most often they were "good news" folks, like grandparents or the milk truck with its clanging milk cans. In the winter, however, the dreaded snow monster appeared during every storm. It always came in the night, first with a growing "clickity clickity clack," and then a single eye appearing on the horizon. Its stare, dulled by falling snow, strengthened as it approached. It marched forward as if coming to get my sister Susie and me, who stood peering through the hole we had breathed in the frost on that big window.

A "snow monster" on our road, circa 1935. (From the collection of Stanley & Elaine Fitch)

When it reached our yard, we could see its huge square form, punctuated by a stern-looking, pointed face. It had long wings that "elbowed" tons of snow out of its way. We shuddered when it reached our yard and stopped. Two men emerged from its bowels with the eerie clank of a steel door. They leaned against the monster's side and relieved themselves. As they lingered and talked, we saw them drinking from a common bottle. Finally, they climbed up and disappeared back inside. The snow monster revved and did a painful about-face. We watched as it

The "gaping snow tunnel where the road had once been." (From the collection of Stanley & Elaine Fitch)

crept back to the horizon, leaving a gaping snow tunnel where the road had once been.

Now that I'm a grown man I know the snow monster was nothing more than a common bulldozer with some added appendages. Back then bulldozers were the weapons of choice in the war against "steeple high" snowstorms. Calais used its trusty TD-14. According to my cousin, who used to drive the thing, it took two days of hard labor to attach the steel framework, V-plow and wings. When that work was all done, the bulldozer was completely metamorphosed, like a friendly butterfly to an ugly caterpillar. It spent that ugly stage crawling the ninety plus miles of Calais winter roads.

My cousin said two men usually plowed, one to operate the wings and the other to drive the machine. One time the road commissioner, who had a drinking problem, headed out alone. He was plowing south on County Road toward Montpelier. He knew the Calais part, even intoxicated, and skillfully "winged" the snow away from every Calais driveway. When he got to the East Montpelier line, however, he was so drunk that he kept right on going. Driveways were unfamiliar in this foreign territory and he pushed huge walls of snow into every one of them. I suspect the two towns fought for years over the runaway snowplower.

All that's left for me are memories, and one old snow monster that still sits at an equipment dealership in Barre. The dealer now sells speedy dump trucks with streamlined plows. Life's answer to modern snowstorms is plowing one lane at a time, fast, and sober! The lone snow monster sits neglected, last in a row of yellow bulldozers and plow parts. It serves to highlight the great evolution of snow removal. I wonder if Susie and I would have been less frightened, way back then, had we known the monster was just a bulldozer dressed for winter. No, I think not —to us it was a snow monster, real and bigger than life, just like the snowstorms we used to know. ✳

Party Poopers and Porcupines

The holidays are over and now we are really into skiing at the Morse Farm. Our cross-country ski center is a giant success. We spent the last year with chain saws, excavators, bulldozers, and bull strength. The grand result is a super ski center with sweeping down hills and banked up curves. People love it. It's quickly becoming one of the most popular Nordic centers in Vermont. In fact, my father Harry, is looking down from heaven as I write with a grin from ear to ear.

You see, Harry Morse wanted to do this ski project thirty years ago but there was a certain 'party pooper' and 'burr' in his side saying, "Dad, we work seven days a week and have one slow season…we're not going to mess up our slow season with a ski center." Yes, that 'Burr' was me, but old age has finally brought me to a place where ski centers are okay. This center's for you Dad, and we're down here havin' a ball with it.

The other day, I was out grooming the trails. Grooming has been a good job for a farmer like me because it involved driving a machine round and round through the countryside. Toward the end of my duties, I was feeling a little tired and saddle worn. As I rounded the last bend, there in the middle of the trail was an ugly old porcupine, just sitting there taking up space. Knowing there were skiers nearby, I viewed Mr. Porky as the opposite of "trail enhancement," possibly providing such dubious perks as rabies and non-prescribed acupuncture. Lacking any rational plan, I broke a stick off from the side of the trail, approached the critter, and gently prodded him. My fears of rabies were at once assuaged and the fellow seemed to be trying to communicate a friendly message, however lost in translation—my French is borderline and my Porcupine nonexistent.

After a fashion, he stirred and waddled off the side of the trail, leaving a distinct porcupine furrow in the deep snow. It was something else he left, however, that finalized the message. "Dear Sir," he was saying, "right now I am relieving myself and if you will kindly stop prodding me with that stick, I will leave when I am done!" I got back on the grooming machine pleased that porky and I were able to resolve our differences with diplomacy. Feeling Dad's presence more than ever, I headed on home thinkin' about party poopers, porky poopers and world-class ski centers. ❧

Swingin' and Swayin'

I just returned from an invigorating, first ski over the new trails we built this past summer. My favorite was the "Frog Run." We based most of our trail names on the maple theme (Sugar Loop, Fancy Loop, Sap Run—you get the drip—uh, drift). As you know, "Frog Run" is also a maple term. After my ski today, however, I wished we had chosen a more historical name than "Frog Run." The Frog Run, you see, winds circuitously around the old Higgins Place, so circuitously it almost makes you dizzy. I aptly thought of old Smolon Higgins as I wound those curves. Smolon would approve of his home place being part of a cross-country ski center. You see, Smolon was a non-conformist—he'd do just about anything with his farm in lieu of milking cows. Shortly after inheriting the place, he installed a hardwood floor in the cow barn and hung up his shingle: "Higgins Barn Dances—Swing and Sway up Higgins' Way." From that point on, there was plenty of swingin' and swayin', and Smolon was the champion swayer. Smolon was rarely sober.

I remember him as a big man. His huge, red face sported a broad, cleft chin, and lived under a western Stetson hat. He was always smiling, a happy drunk. His best friend was a huge Packard automobile that not only accompanied him on his rounds, but took on a persona of its own. "The Old Packard" was the perfect scapegoat when Smolon ended up off the road or over a bridge. Once when I was young, we were awakened at 3 A.M. by Nipper. He bayed with deafening

Cummings Barn up by Frog Run ski trail.

concern, but then mysteriously quieted. When my father went to the kitchen to investigate, he discovered Smolon sitting at our kitchen table, Stetson placed aside, and a red bandana tucked into his collar, bib style. He was eating some raw venison steak and feeding morsels to an ecstatic Nipper.

"Evnin' Harry", he slurred. "Th'old Packard juss wanned t'pull intayur driveway. W'heard ya gottadeer t'day an' b'God we foun some in th'ref-ffrijrater!"

My father had, indeed, shot a deer earlier and stocked the refrigerator with fresh venison.

"Hello Smolon," he said, probably hiding a big grin. "I'm glad you like my deer meat. When you go out, be sure to turn off the lights." With that, Smolon gave a broad, toothy grin, saluted with the dexterity of an octopus, and resumed his meal.

Smolon Higgins and his old Packard faded away about the same time, liver and rust the weak links. The barn still sports that hardwood floor, now home to some stored items and an occasional pick-up basketball game. Our ski trails go quite close to that barn, winding around the ledges and new growth maple trees.

Smolon's memory is largely gone, along with the old maples, but I remember him. Yessir, I remember. He was good to my dog and never really hurt anyone. Darn. I wish we'd named those trails, "Smolon's Way." ❧

In a Pickle

Last weekend I went skiing with my friends Nat and Earl. The trails were blessed with good grooming, good weather, and a striking whiteness. It had snowed just enough to give personality to the trees and attitude to our skis. Morse Farm Ski Touring's motto, "the sweetest ski in Vermont," fit like a warm glove that day. We headed up the Fancy Loop, on our way to the Maple Trail at a pace pleasing to our "mid-fifty" frames. Cross-country skiing is friendly that way, you know. Our trail system winds like a long ribbon around the hills and valleys of the Morse Farm. It affords a good chance for sociability on the uphills and "air-against-your-face" thrills on the downhills. For some reason, the physics of cross-country skiing usually err in favor of the uphills, or so it seems. That leaves fewer thrills and lots of time for talk. Our subjects varied from aches and pains to baling wire, but the three of us, a Republican, a Democrat and a 'sort of,' eventually "herringboned" right into talk of politics. We didn't really agree on anything, but who cares. When you're skiing, you can't fight.

We followed each other, shirttail to shirttail, down the final hills on the Maple

Trail, bringing the talk of politics to an abrupt halt. We skied on toward the open meadows in the Sugar Loop and sunshine. Nat and Earl had a mid-afternoon date with the New England Patriots, so we turned north toward the ski center. Sweat was beginning to speak from my inner layers when we reached the parking lot. As we stood there agreeing that life is good, something white streaked past our feet. We looked toward some black culverts that are stored nearby and there, poking its tiny head out from one, was a snow white weasel. He looked at us with friendly, dark eyes and then strolled right on over. I looked down as he circled my boots. He looked clean and healthy, and he meant no harm. After a quick inspection, he about-faced and pattered a few feet away to a small hole in the snow. There he nonchalantly reached down, picked up a fat rodent, and carried it back to the culvert.

Years ago, some neighbors of ours had a weasel in their house. I once heard that means good luck. Those folks loved their little weasel because he got rid of their mice and besides that, well, he was just a friendly guy. He stayed relatively subdued, but occasionally came out to the living area to socialize. Sometimes they teased him with a piece of liver on a string. He danced and rolled like a kitten. One day they found their little friend in the pickle barrel, floating in the brine. He had gone for his salt fix and, well, you might say, "gotten into a pickle." They placed their little departed friend in the freezer. I would, too, if he really meant good luck. They admitted, when the harvest came in that year, they had to throw him out to make room for something else.

I'll never forget our little 'ski weasel.' He "high-tailed" it across the yard with his meal in his mouth about the time my friends left for the ball game. I think he did bring good luck that day—how can you argue that when everything ends so well, even politics! 🍁

The Psychology of Tree Season

As I have said in the past, we maple sugarmakers do lots of things to make a living here in Vermont because the sugar season is only four or five weeks long. In fact, our curse up here in God's country might just be the seasons—not the shortage of, but the shortness of. Our seasons are plentiful. We have four to be exact (five, if you count mud season), but they're so short we can hardly finish the current one's work when the next one arrives. Now we're into Christmas tree season and what a nail chewer that one is! Have you ever tried to sell a Christmas tree on December 26? I mean, unlike wine, Christmas trees do not improve with age.

My good friend Deb put it another way. "Growing up on a Christmas tree farm in North Carolina, I know just how beautiful it can be. The people, yes, they have to have a little bit of angel in them or maybe some type of forest imp or fairy to manicure and tend the trees, all for that one special cutting once a year." Thanks, Deb. I do feel like a Christmas Tree Imp sometimes as I help people pick out their trees. A few days ago was one of those times.

Christmas trees for sale at Morse Farm.

The man was dressed to the hilt and bent on a mission; he needed the perfect Christmas tree. He shared the yard with several other tree shoppers, including one little old lady with a "Vermont-wise" look. I watched from a distance as "Mr. Clean" directed the young man who worked for me to whirl and twirl every tree for careful inspection. He poked and prodded with no glimpse of approval on his face. All the while he made comments like: "it needs to be full-bodied, but not too full...there's a sort of softness I'm looking for," and, "that one has a complexion problem, but it has a small butt like I need." With his last comment, the little old lady who had been eavesdropping, strutted over and boomed, "Young man, you're not marrying the damned thing...it's only a Christmas tree!" Then she retreated to a scrubby little tree with a bad complexion, but lots of personality. In a much softer tone, she said, "Tie this one up for me, it's just right."

I smiled a big Tree Imp smile, and Mr. Clean finally selected his tree.

I'm sure it will be his best tree ever and expect to witness the same ritual next year. I love the psychology of Christmas tree shopping. With thirty-two years of experience, I'm almost a Ph.D. and there's one thing above all else I've learned— it takes all types to make the world go around. 🍁

The Psychology of Tree Season 2

Last year at this time I wrote "The Psychology of Tree Season." Since it's tree season again, I figure a sequel is in order. This one came to me the other day as I drove my tractor up County Road with a twelve-foot Christmas tree suspended from the bucket loader. I had received a note that Mr. and Mrs. Hallowell would be here to pick up their usual twelve-foot tree that night. The Hallowells are a cute, elderly couple who've been coming to our place for years. Mrs. Hallowell loves her Christmas trees, especially twelve-foot ones. That makes Mrs. Hallowell an enigma. You see, it's almost universal that the older folks get, the smaller their tree becomes. Not so Mrs. Hallowell. In fact, she's the only exception I can think of in thirty-three years in this business. That afternoon, I donned my snow gear, loaded up the chainsaw, and aimed my tractor and trailer for the Christmas tree lot.

I quickly found a tree that looked about twelve-feet tall (real Vermonters don't carry tape measures) and lopped it off. I dragged it out and wrestled it onto the trailer. Sure enough, it measured an exact twelve feet against the ten-foot trailer bed. Then I went and found another one. "I gotta give Mrs. Hallowell a choice," I thought, knowing some young person would buy the second tree. I started up the chainsaw and reached far into the second tree's middle. It toppled softly, cushioned by the broad, dense boughs. I grabbed hold and dragged it toward the rig. It pulled hard and proved impossible to load onto the trailer with the other one. This tree was a beauty—and massive! My Yankee mind turned to the bucket loader and some quick riggin'. Soon, I was headed back to the store with that huge tree hanging from the loader like a brandy barrel from a St. Bernard.

The Hallowells arrived sometime after dark and had already selected the smaller tree when I was called. As I approached, Mr. Hallowell was cinching the boughs back for transport. I said my hellos and started helping all at the same time. We had just wrestled the thing onto the top of their Toyota station wagon when the Mrs. returned from paying.

"I'm surprised you didn't select the other tree, Mrs. Hallowell," I said. "It is much fuller than the one you took."

She turned to me purposefully and scolded, "Burr Morse, I come to Morse Farm for quality and service. I don't come here to get 'supersized'!" With that they thanked me, got into that familiar Toyota and headed down the road. I sold that big beautiful tree the next day. It went to a seventy-five-year-old woman who walked with a cane—I stand corrected! 🍁

Seasonal Talk

Our neighborhood moose.

There's such a magical feeling to this time of year, not that it's all rosy. Sometimes I have to throw in a little marriage counseling with the Christmas trees. Overall though, folks are operating at maximum speed and spirits, and it's so good to have some snow to mix with the fragrance of fresh balsam and the colored lights—snow, balsam and colored lights—quite a contrast from the sand, palm trees, and stars at that original Christmas. I'm not complaining, though; I couldn't imagine Christmas any other way.

One thing we have that does fit the original mold is the manger and the animals. I grew up with a big barn full of farm animals that, to this day, drives my nostalgia like eight tiny reindeer. Legend has it that the animals "talk" at the stroke of midnight on Christmas Eve. I've always been a true believer; however, I never did get out to the barn at midnight to hear them. Now, fifty years later, I realize why I avoided it—I was afraid of what the cusses might say about me!

Animals truly do talk to us. My mother is ninety-years-old and has had terrible back pain lately. She spends her days alone in her recliner, concerned about the cause of her back pain.

The other day my brother, Tick, came to visit. She roused and asked about a dark lump which had been in her other recliner for some time. The "lump," it seemed, was a big fat mouse that sat facing the TV as if intent on the program. Tick instinctively grabbed a broom and lunged after Mr. Mouse, who lunged to all corners of the living room, one swat ahead of the broom. The mouse finally found safety behind a bookcase and hasn't been seen since. My mother, besides finding it great entertainment, said she felt a "presence" before Tick came. She joked that the mouse had come to keep her company. I'm convinced he did and his message was this: "Don't worry, Dot, everything will be alright."

A few days ago I sold a Christmas tree to some neighbors who were recently visited by a small, bull moose. They saw him coming—said he first stopped and pruned their lilac bush. He then proceeded to the hedgerow only twelve feet from their picture window. The Moose was so close they spotted porcupine quills sticking in the back of his head. The husband grabbed his camera and went right out. He got pictures fit for *Vermont Life* of young "Bullwinkle," who just blinked and continued his pruning. I'm convinced Bullwinkle's visit went beyond gastric fulfillment. He came with a message about those quills:

"Look, I encountered a porcupine who lacked the Christmas spirit. If these quills were in any other part of my body I could deal with them, but they're in the back of my head for heaven's sake!"

Those are just two examples of animal talk and human response. I'm not blaming Tick for grabbing the broom or my neighbor for not grabbing his tweezers. No, they were just following their instincts and animals usually follow theirs. There are times, however, when all creatures use a universal language, instincts be damned. One time my father helped a skunk whose head was stuck in a jar. My father stroked the skunk's back and lulled him into relaxation, such total relaxation that peace, alone, powered him out of that jar. The skunk thanked my father—yes, he did. He did it with his eyes. If the message is "peace" or "love," any language will do, even a squeak or a hee-haw. Peace be with you. 🍁

Secret Silos and World Class Wreaths

The last of our foliage buses have gone back down County Road, my leaves are raked, and there is snow in the air. Roads, leaves, snow. Kinda makes me think about Robert Frost, fellow Vermonter, and great hero of mine. I'm thinking, especially, of his "Road Not Taken" poem:

> *"Two roads diverged in a wood, and I—*
> *I took the one less traveled by,*
> *And that has made all the difference"*

Wow! Such profound and universal words. We all have a "less traveled road that has made all the difference" in our lives. The one I think of now is the road to Vermont's Northeast Kingdom, the road that leads to our new wreath maker, Jacinthe, from up in Lemington. We were so sold on the quality of Jacinthe's wreaths that we ordered another bunch for this year and I looked forward to my next trip up that less traveled road.

Last year Tessa and I made a real occasion of that trip. I packed our supper, a turkey sandwich for me and a can of Alpo for her. We headed north with the Morse Farm van late on a snowy November day. Thinking of the hectic foliage season that had just ended, I was glad to be on the road. We stopped by a river to eat, and both agreed, "It doesn't get any better than this." I reviewed my directions as I ate. Somewhere on the left, there would be a "Luke's Body Shop" and a green ranch house, directions adequate for a man and a beagle with all the time in the world. We finished our suppers and continued north on Vt. 102.

I held the words "Luke's Body Shop" close in my mind. We drove on, November's edgy personality showing through pulsating wiper blades. I suspected we had gone too far when the French speaking signs became thick, like the hair on Tessa's back. That notion was abruptly confirmed by a red sign that stood starkly in our path bearing the word 'Arret' (French for 'Stop'). I realized Canadian Customs was directly in front of me. Tessa and I looked at each other, her head tilted in that beagle way as if to say, "What now?" We turned around and retraced our path until we saw an inviting homestead on the right. I stopped the van, got out and walked past two friendly plywood geese holding the name "St. Onge." Before I could knock, a small, graying woman opened the door.

Luc Marchesseault's body shop—good friend, bi-linguist, and Christmas tree grower extraordinaire.

"Bonjour," she said. "I see you go by—dat brightly let-terd van you drive. You look loss."

"I am," I said, and handed her my directions to Luke's Body Shop. "You mean Luc's Body Shop!" she said, both of us now laughing at my stupid mistake. I remembered going by a building with the word "Luc's" on a sign.

"You da man from Montpel-yey who buys rete from Jacinthe?" I said I was, now knowing there were no secrets in the Kingdom.

"Jacinthe make da bess rete in all Vermont. Dey lass till July. I tink da se-cret is in da si-low."

At that point, Tessa started a lively conversation with the St. Onge dog. I quickly thanked Mrs. St. Onge and leapt for the van, hoping to curtail a canine war. Somewhere in the process, I misplaced her last words.

We arrived at Jacinthe's place to find a friendly Luc and Jacinthe waiting by their pick-up truck, our imminent arrival obviously reported by Mrs. St. Onge. After we exchanged pleasantries, they beckoned me out back of the body shop. There lay a large pile of wreaths inside a circular foundation that was recessed in the ground. The place used to be a farm, they explained, and the foundation formerly supported a silo. The wreaths, they said, stayed fresher and greener below ground level inside the old silo. Soon we had loaded all 400 wreaths into my van, leaving just enough room for a man and a small dog to scrunch together, honeymoon style.

Our ride home was enriched with the scent of balsam. The snow had stopped falling and as we rolled south into the night, I thought of 400 fluffy wreaths on 400 doors all over the U.S.A. They each sported a bright red bow and natural cones from the North Woods. They were deep, balsam green and they stayed fresh, seemingly forever. That I knew, because Mrs. St. Onge had told me, "the secret is in the silo." 🍁

Two Sounds of Sugarin'

It had been an unusual sugar season. Starting three weeks early with our necessary freezing nights and thawing days, it brought about a week of a good old-fashioned sap run, then froze back up solid. We waited anxiously for its return and I knew that was about to happen when I started hearing those train whistles down at Montpelier Junction. Even though the junction is six miles from Morse Farm, as the crow flies, an approaching storm will make those old train whistles sound like they are next door. During sugarin', that's always good news because, as I have said, sugarmakers thrive on ornery weather.

Sure enough, I rolled out of bed the next morning and looked out to a world of sticky snowflakes as big around as quarters. They descended like feathers and melted on touchdown, a phenomenon known to sugarmakers as 'sugar snow'. The wind was out of the west, the temperature was thirty-six degrees and the sap ran wicked fast! By mid-morning, steam rolled out of our sugarhouse and barrels filled with great flavored Grade A Medium Amber maple syrup.

A distant sound forecasted the good run. However, the end of our season was near. We know that because of the sound of frogs—spring peepers—those little rascals from the swamp that serenaded our nights with their soothing chorus.

Our next sap run will be the 'Frog Run'—sounds like a marathon for amphibians, but it's really the term for the final breath of sugarin'. After that we wash up, get on with the next season, and dream about a time when the world is all snowy again and it is time to tap the trees. 🍁

(Jackie Tollmann Photo)

"Man in Woodpile."

Mud Season Magic

Our trees are finally all tapped. Whew! We spent a lot of the pre-season on snowshoes, walkin' through some tough snow conditions. Right after the tapping was finished, our weather was too warm. We prayed for a cooldown. We peered skyward as if to make some kind of sugarmaker-to-celestial connection. Then it turned cold—too cold for a sap run! Remember that famous "Howard Dean Scream?" I think he learned that scream from a frustrated Vermont maple sugarmaker!

Today the sap is running, finally. I stand here cold and shivering, boiling sap and writing at the same time. Droplets of condensed steam splash onto my notepad from the tin sugarhouse roof. The thermometer outside says thirty-four degrees, normally too cold for a sap run. I look over at a round glass vacuum jar that rests in a tangle of piping and gauges, a "Rube Goldberg" device, new to our sugarhouse. Sap gushes into the jar from trees up above the sugarhouse. Today the jar fills quickly and empties often into the storage tank. I'm making a nice light-colored Fancy Grade syrup—pleased that sap will run on this cold day and somewhat more understanding of "why" after talking to my last sugarhouse visitor. He walked in, face elevated toward the rising steam, nose twitching slightly, a Vermonter to the core.

"Fancy, b'God," he declared.

"Yup," I agreed.

"Knew th't you'd be boilin' today—-mud roads start—sap'll run, weather be damned,' he spurted like the sap coming into my jar.

I nodded, too busy to speak.

Translated, his message spoke of a certain communication between the frost and the trees and the change of seasons. When the back roads surrender to winter's frost and cars get stuck in the mud, sap runs. Period.

It brought memories from my youth of back roads and walking home from the Center School. We stopped at muddy spots and sank down to the top of our boots, argued all the time about how fast quicksand will "suck you right under." Then to the rallying cry of, "beat you to the jelly roll," we'd run on to a place where the whole road undulated with the bouncing of our eighty-pound bodies. We'd eventually get home to upset mothers and a steamy sugarhouse. Those were the days! 🍁

That Glorious Fragrance

Whew! It's been one of those years where preparation for sugarin' has been a real stretch. Thank God, my boys, Rob and Tom, stepped in and finished the job fast while I went to work getting the sugarhouse ready. That's always the problem with the sugarhouse having sat idle for eleven months out. There was a lot of washing and organizing to do. The evaporator needed to be washed and leveled. Sap boils at just one inch deep, so level is very important. After considerable adjustment, I was ready to fire her up.

First, I flooded the whole thing with an inch of sap and then touched a match to the wood. Praying applied at this point as leaks are always frustrating and sometimes terminal to the process. Thankfully, there were none. My job then was to wait for boiling to start, followed by that glorious fragrance of sweetness.

You know, eleven months is a long time to wait for that fragrance and for a Vermont sugarmaker, it is, without a doubt, the highlight of the year. That fragrance seeps into every pore, gets in our blood, and is, indeed, part of our DNA. I have a friend, Ron, who used to sugar in Jericho. Through divorce and circumstances, he is now in Portland, Oregon, but walks around with Vermont DNA. He pines for sugarin' and when he visits our website, Ron will smell sap boiling, I'm sure.

So far this season, I have made ninety gallons of syrup and our sugar content has been high. Sometimes drought (as we experienced last summer) causes a sweeter sap and so far that theory prevails. Right now, it is only taking thirty-four gallons of sap to make one gallon of syrup and it is much easier to make light colored syrup with a sweet sap. Most of those ninety gallons have been Fancy Grade.

We are waiting for the next run right now. Winter has returned, but that is good news. Sugarmaking is 95% nature and 5% man. Essential for a sap run are freezing nights, thawing days, and preferably a west wind. As I made my point earlier: good weather is bad for sugarmakers and bad weather is good. We love wet, sticky spring snowstorms, the kind that snap telephone lines and bend birches earthward, because they bring us another run of sap. This cold spell we are now waiting out, will do just that.

Speaking of the cold spell, our crust returned. This morning, I walked through the pasture from my house to work. The combination of gravity and very slippery crust suddenly brought me to a full fledged and quite graceful glide. Everything was going quite swimmingly (or skiingly) until I struck a rough snow bank at the bottom of the slope. Down I went, right on my bad shoulder. I'm okay. I know the power of that sugarhouse steam and expect a miraculous recovery, quick and sweet. 🍁

Sugar season at Morse Farm— no snow but steam rising.

(Jackie Tollmann Photo)

Cool Sugarin'

Today, spring is showing its fickle side to us sugarmakers. We have been boiling away "to beat the band," but I am looking out the window to the North at snow coming down fast, listening to the cars creep by on County Road, and feeling like a time machine has swept us back into January. Sugarin' has gone away for the moment, but it will return. A good blizzard will postpone the season, but will also stimulate it. When the weather moderates, sap runs will return with sweet vengeance. In the meantime, we are happy with frozen ruts and sap icicles, awaiting the return of our beloved sugar season.

I had many visitors in the sugarhouse last week when I was boiling. My favorite one of all was a smiling, round-faced girl of about ten. I took an instant shine to her as mother led her in through the steam. They stepped up on the riser and peered into the front pan.

"Cool," she said, smiling.

I explained how the sweetened sap enters from the back pan and flows up and down through the front pan maze, sweetening as it goes along.

"Cool," she said, smiling more.

I explained how finished maple syrup boils at seven degrees above the boiling point of water.

"Cool."

At that very instant, I was filling the hydrometer cup with hot syrup to show her how specific gravity plays in and spilled some on my thumb. Not wanting to look unprofessional, I held my tongue, gritted my teeth and finished the task.

"Cool," she said as they walked toward the door.

Thinking they were gone, I did an agonized pirouette followed by three quick sugarhouse stomps, but mother and daughter had turned around and had seen my antics.

"What was that for?" the girl asked.

"Oh, it's, ah, just my sap dance," I invented. "You know, sort of like a rain dance."

To that, her smile thickened like maple syrup. "COOL!" she said.

That night as my blisters were speaking, "hot, hot, hot," I managed a chuckle over that happy little girl. Her smile warmed my day in more ways than one, but my memory will forever be etched with one word. Cool. 🍁

Peace with Pickles

Today, my son Tom, and I were down in the South End tapping trees. It's been a little tough this year with all the cold weather, but today was different. We worked under a bright blue sky brimming with white clouds. Though not quite sap weather, the temperature was not bad—not bad at all. Our cross-country ski trail traversed the sugarbush right where we worked.

Some of the skiers swished by as though they had a deadline to make. Others slowed to exchange pleasantries. The skiers added a social dimension to an already pleasant day. Two of the "swishers" were employees of our ski center, Pavel, a young Russian, and Terry, originally from Connecticut. Tom and I chuckled at their fleeting, "Hi guys, how are ya?" as the next bend swallowed them up.

You see, Pavel and Terry are of the modern cross-country ski breed, skaters. Skaters have no time to stop.

We resumed our tapping. Tom wielded the noisy little engine drill and I pounded spouts.

We are behind, I thought, sugar weather will wake up one day soon and we must be ready. I focus on the distant tree line where our job would end for the day. Beyond that lay the rest of the world, clear to Connecticut, and Russia. Besides maple sugaring, my thoughts dwell on that world; I conclude Vermont is a place where we've figured it all out. In Vermont, skaters and sugarers can live in harmony.

At the end of the day we piled our gear on the snowmobile sled and headed back to the store. Sugar-on-snow was still being served and we hurried to get ours. Down we sat with our dishes of snow, cups of maple syrup, raised donuts and dill pickles—hog heaven for Vermonters like us. We drizzled syrup in circular patterns over the snow, balled it up with a fork, and bit generously into the unsweetened yeast donuts. Then came the pickles; those glorious, crunchy pickles made instant peace with the sweetness in our mouths. Peace. Peace? My mind went out on a creative limb—those pickles aren't supposed to get along with the maple syrup, but they do. Wow!

Tom and I retired to our homes, tired from the day and full of our farm's sweetness. My final thoughts before slumber that night were of the big world again; a world where pickles and maple syrup reign and everyone is happy. ❧

Front Pan Marriage

February 4 and Sugarin' 2003 was fast approaching. Yesterday, we ordered a new front pan for our evaporator. Front pans are the finishing end of an evaporator, where the final stage of all our hard labor trickles out as golden, pure maple syrup. Before evaporators, there were single pots over open fires and before that there were Indians with birch bark vessels; before that, well, "Let there be light…"

As you know, boiling sap is a long and arduous project. It normally takes forty gallons of sap to boil into one gallon of maple syrup. Back in the "open pot" days, sap was constantly being poured in to replenish what was leaving as steam. Because of the dilution factor, the darned stuff took forever to get done. Finally, some creative old Yankee said, "enough is enough," and invented the evaporator. An evaporator acts as a river, where pure sap starts in the back, boils as it travels through baffles, and pure syrup comes out the front.

Our old front pan had sadly and silently suffered the warping and racking of heat, but being twenty-years-old, owed us nothing. It was a traditional style front pan which required a reversal of its flow daily to control the sugar stone or niter deposit that came with boiling. In our sugarhouse, that meant I had to "syrup off" (draw syrup) from the backside of the evaporator every other day, the side away from our lights and sugarhouse door. Many times in the past, I went home at night and declared to Betsy that my day had been dark. I had been on the "far side" that day!

(Jackie Tollmann Photo)

Burr in sugarhouse, Spring, 2003.

Our new front pan system is a modern configuration which will allow syruping off to always be on the front side, a place much more amenable to greeting groups of sugarhouse visitors. I am really looking forward to it!

For a multi-generation sugarmaker like me, the front pan is the heart and soul of sugarin'. It is where the boiling sap finally turns to the frothing sweetness that smells wonderful and sheets thickly off the edge of a dipper. It is the place where nature meets economics and the palate is happy.

Speaking of 'happy,' my father used to equate my mother to the action in the front pan. "The sap travels back and forth through the baffles, getting sweeter as it goes, just like my wife, Dot, has over the last fifty years."

We are itchin' for sugarin' to start and especially to try out that new front pan. Sugarin' is a lot of work, but we always hope for sap runs that keep us busy 'round the clock. At those times, Betsy brings my meals to the sugarhouse and forgives my usual household chores. Betsy, by the way, has gotten sweeter and sweeter with time, too. I better say that, lest I end up on the dark side! ❧

Sugarhouse Music

On the eve of the last day of Sugarin' 2003, I was amazed at what a nail chewer of a season this one was. It started out late because of the cold, then the weather turned too warm and sluggish. We felt our season slipping away and needed a storm, a good old-fashioned sugarin' snowstorm! Two weeks into the feeble season, our "storm" prayers were answered with a sudden and fierce return to winter. Winter bared its ugly teeth for almost two weeks putting sugarin' on hold for that long stretch. Finally, winter moderated and we got a rip-roaring, old-fashioned sap run at the end. We made a good volume, thanks to that final run. It was dark syrup, but most folks like dark syrup better, anyway. The weatherman is hinting at seventy-degree days for a while now and seventy-degree weather fits Vermont sugarin' about like a saddle fits a hog. Sugarin's done.

We have many sugarhouse visitors in the course of each season and one small boy stood out particularly this year. He came walking in one day with his mother.

I was intent on my boiling and listening to the local 'Oldies Rock and Roll' station. The sugarhouse atmosphere was stunning that day. White, billowy steam embodied the luscious maple fragrance as mother and son strolled in. The sounds of 'I Want to Hold Your Hand' mixed pleasantly with the crackling fire. At once I heard the boy's small voice say, "Mom, that's Sugarhouse Music!"

The words "Sugarhouse Music" brought on déjà vu as powerfully as the sap was running that day.

Let me explain: the job of boilin' can get boring. I remember the long hours spent with my father in our sugarhouse. Nipper lay curled up under the big wood-fired arch, soakin' up all that heat. I hauled wood in from the shed and Father drew off batches of maple syrup. For two Vermonters with sugarin' in their blood, that's all romantic stuff. At midnight, however, when you're bone tired from fourteen hours of sugarin' and still have a tank full of sap yet to boil, the romance just kinda wears out.

For times like that, we had the radio. The radio was our soul mate, confidante, and preserver of sanity. My father's favorite was EZ Listening music on WEZF, a.k.a., "elevator music." He had no use for my favorite, Rock and Roll—calling it "gosh darned cat-a-wallin'!" My friend, Paul Cate, named Father's choice, "Sugarhouse Music" since it was always playing.

I have to admit, EZ Listening is fine with me at this stage of the game. It is, however, hard to find any stations that play it these days. In fact, most of the stuff you hear on the radio now is GOSH DARNED CAT-A-WALLIN'! So, I hereby deem "Oldies, Rock and Roll" the new replacement, sort of by default. The point of this story is that nothing really changes in our sugarhouse. Sure, both Father and Nipper have gone on to a warm, sweet place in the sky, but they're looking down on the same old Morse sugarhouse; a steamy place where every drop of maple syrup is blessed by "Sugarhouse Music." 🍁

Sweet Wisdom

We're nearing the end of our maple sugar season. This year, Murphy's Law called the shots. We had everything from too cold, to too warm, to the wrong wind direction. As you know, weather in Vermont can be ornery. Because I'm a Yankee, I'll never accept defeat; if I can't "crack" a case, I'll at least worry it to death.

My queries have led to numerous sugarhouse conversations. Here were a couple of the more creative ideas.

One seasoned Vermonter blamed NASA; said it was "them rockets they keep sendin' up there." He went on to say if God meant us to be fooling around in space, He'd have at least put maple trees on the moon.

The guy who helps me in the sugarhouse thought it was a curse. Not just any curse, but The Boston Red Sox's Curse of the Bambino. His theory was that the Curse, being energy, couldn't just disappear. It simply followed the path of least

resistance and traveled three hours north to the Vermont maple industry. We boiled sap one day when he expressed his thoughts. Our speculation got quite creative:

"You mean we have eighty-five consecutive no-win seasons to go?" I asked, thinking again of sugarin' on the moon. He nodded in the affirmative, suggesting there was not a thing we could do.

"Can't even buy more expensive team trees," he said. "If it's the Curse, nothing'll break it."

I had just suggested possibly feeding steroids to our maple trees when an older man entered the sugarhouse. We welcomed him and explained why we were laughing. He saw the humor and then narrowed his eyes. Turning toward me he said:

"I came in last year and you boasted of a great season, didn't you?"

"Yes," I said, wondering what he was getting at.

"You're foolish to question a bad season," he counseled, and then used an expression I'd never heard: "The years teach you what the days never know." With that, he took a long whiff of the boiling sap, did a brisk about-face and left.

The wisdom of his message reminded me of two experiences I'd had a few days earlier:

In the past I've been a "night worrier," but have lately been learning techniques to nip the pesky problem in the bud. The other night I woke up with worries about the bad sugar season, but quickly put my new learning to work and went back to sleep. It was 6:00 A.M. when I woke for the day and there, framed by the glass door on the south side of my bedroom, sat a plump barred owl. He scanned the valley from his white birch perch thinking of breakfast, I suppose. Occasionally, his huge eyes swiveled in my direction, making direct contact with my own. I felt honored to start my day in the company of this guy, the universal symbol of wisdom.

The next night I had less success in taming my worries. I rose at 6:00 again, feeling tired and grumpy. I just started to dress when I noticed the dark form of a turkey moving from the distant treeline out into the white snow. Another one followed and then another, I counted six in all, strutting single file across my line of view. As they disappeared into last year's cornfield, the symbolism of it all hit me: My good night gave me an owl for wisdom; my bad night gave me turkeys for stupidity.

This morning, I woke to the same old sugar season, but with a little different attitude. I thought of a world where the owls and turkeys roamed free and people critiqued from a closed corral. I knew we'd get through this season of days. It's the years that count. ❧

Dot Morse's Tribute to her Father

The little tow-haired fellow slid down from his feather bed, rubbed the sleepy seeds out of his eyes, pulled on his pants, and headed barefoot for the pasture to bring in old Smiley for the morning milking.

He'd done this every morning almost since he could remember and he was almost seven now.

But he loved the early morning when the sun was just beginning to rise and the valley below became a sea of fog.

And he especially loved going after old Smiley, not because he particularly loved old Smiley, but because he loved the little things along the way.

In the spring, there were the Hepaticas and the Adder's Tongues in the woods and on the edge of the pasture. In the summer came the Black-Eyed Susans and Queen Anne's Lace. In the fall, the Goldenrod and the turning leaves.

And always, just a few steps out of his way, the Old Oak Tree—his greatest friend, the one he could go to when no one understood him. The Old Oak heard about it; the big kids in the little red schoolhouse a half mile away who stole his lunch-pail chocolate cake day after day until he learned to eat it first—and save the sandwiches for later.

It was only the Old Oak who knew how much he had wanted to go to college after high school. Everybody else just thought he wanted to start his berry farm.

It was to this leafy friend that he brought his shy, dark-eyed bride, and it was just barely beyond its shadows that they built their (one and only) home—a home from which four little children eventually made their own well-worn paths to the Old Oak where they began to tell and listen to secrets, while the now grown-up little tow-head went on to become well-known in Montpelier and in Washington, helping to make laws for his state and country—but always in such a way that the Old Oak Tree could never be ashamed of anything he said or anything he did.

The years changed him; the years changed the Old Oak—but only outwardly. Recognition came to him. The Senator says, "Declare victory and get out of Vietnam." Recognition came to the Old Oak: "Largest oak in state of Vermont." (257 inches in circumference).

Then Father Time stepped in. At his bidding, the man began to walk a little slower, the tree lost a few branches. In the fall of '84, the man was taken far away to a rest home, and the autumn winds broke dozens more branches from the Old Oak.

In his delirium, late in November, the man spoke often of his long-time friend, as if he wanted us all to continue the friendship. As long as he could speak, the Old Oak was on his tongue and, until his death the morning of November 19, in his thoughts.

Winter that year came and went. In the spring we went with a mixture of rememberings and hopings, to the Old Oak Tree on the hill. There it lay—a shattered pile of branches—a silent tribute to a ninety-year-old friendship.

But there in the midst of the broken heap was one long, thin finger of oak wood, pointing upward toward a bright blue sky.

At its feet Spring Beauties nodded in the gentle wind and the blackberry vines gave promise of a good crop.

To the Old Oak Tree and the little tow-haired fellow:

'Requiescat in pace.'

Epilogue

I'm the luckiest guy in the world. I've inherited lots of Vermont savvy from my parents, and you've just read some of the highlights. I'd like to especially thank my mother for the nurturing and for encouraging me to write. It was once said that my mother, teacher supreme, could even teach from the highest branches of a tree. I'd go one step beyond; with her teaching we were like birds, free to fly into the huge world and follow our dreams. I never 'flew' far from Vermont because, well, why leave the best place in the world? My heart's right here and it'll be here after I'm gone—then, no doubt, there'll be someone else, another thin finger of oak, to look ahead toward sweet days and beyond. —*Burr*